Seasons of My Life

The Changing Times That Defined My World

Anne James

Please, step inside...

*I wonder who's knocking at my door,
A friend of old, a treasure to explore.
Please, step inside, take respite from the cold,
Nestle by the hearth, where stories are told.*

*As we fix our gaze upon the dancing blaze,
With whiskey's warmth, our spirits ablaze,
Embracing memories, laughter, tears combined,
In tales of yore, the essence of mankind.*

*Those youthful escapades we lovingly recount,
The daring mischief, adventures paramount.
Our parents' fretting, their worries unfurled,
Yet we emerged unscathed in this vibrant world.*

*Then we delve deep into life's sombre scenes,
Change, loss, grief, and what it all means.
Yet hope, relentless, within us prevails,
That our children shall conquer their own daunting trails.*

*Reflecting upon the tapestry we've sewn,
Assured, our values will endure, fully grown.
Farewell, dear friend, return when stars align,
To wander through time, as wisdom intertwines.*

*For as we age, our wisdom takes flight,
And oh, those stories we have yet to recite.
With fervour, we'll share the treasures we've amassed,
For wisdom blossoms, boundless and unsurpassed.*

- Anne James

First published by Ultimate World Publishing 2023
Copyright © 2023 Anne James

ISBN

Paperback: 978-1-922982-94-0
Ebook: 978-1-922982-95-7

Anne James has asserted her rights under the Copyright, Designs and Patents Act 1988 to be identified as the author of this work. The information in this book is based on the author's experiences and opinions. The publisher specifically disclaims responsibility for any adverse consequences which may result from use of the information contained herein. Permission to use information has been sought by the author. Any breaches will be rectified in further editions of the book.

All rights reserved. No part of this publication may be reproduced, stored in or introduced into a retrieval system, or transmitted in any form, or by any means (electronic, mechanical, photocopying, recording or otherwise) without the prior written permission of the author. Any person who does any unauthorised act in relation to this publication may be liable to criminal prosecution and civil claims for damages. Enquiries should be made through the publisher.

Cover design: Ultimate World Publishing
Layout and typesetting: Ultimate World Publishing
Editor: Victoria Pickens
Cover painting: David Bleakley
Photographer (Author Photos): Melanie de Ruyter
Melanie Kate Creative
@melanie_kate_creative

Ultimate World Publishing
Diamond Creek,
Victoria Australia 3089
www.writeabook.com.au

'Having worked with Anne James for ten years in a country medical practice I know her to be a gentle, caring lady with an encyclopaedic knowledge of community medicine. Whether it was a forty-year-old having a cardiac arrest, or a confused elderly patient who needed immediate emergency nursing home accommodation, in any emergency it was Anne who you wanted working by your side.

So it was with great pleasure that I read Seasons of My Life, the story of how her life has been shaped by both the timeless values of her family and the rapidly changing world she has lived through. A book I would recommend to all.'

Dr Sandra Ward, MBBS, Retired Country GP

'Ours is a friendship that is unbroken for more than four decades. It is built on a foundation of shared experiences, shared values and shared interests. Whilst Anne and I have many aspects of our lives that are individual passions and pursuits, there has been one enduring thread throughout our friendship: words! Our love of the written and spoken word has sustained us through both the celebrations and tragedies of our lives. Now having read the first draft of Seasons of My Life there is only one word that truly describes my feelings about Anne and her beloved first book. Brave, so brave to have undertaken this journey and so eminently brave to have done it with such dignified consideration and honesty. It is my honour to offer this testimonial to the readers of Seasons of My Life, written by my brave friend, Anne.'

Kim Macgowan

Acknowledgement of Country

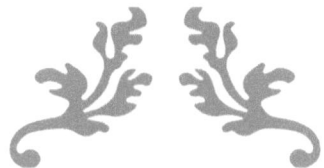

I acknowledge the Traditional Owners and Custodians of Lutruwita and pay my respects to the Elders, past and present.

I thank them for sharing their cultures, spiritualities, storytelling and their ways of living on and with this land that we are all now privileged to call home.

Contents

Acknowledgement of Country	vii
Dedication	1
Introduction	3
Chapter 1: Those Formative Years	9
Chapter 2: A Place to Call Home	21
Chapter 3: Becoming a Nurse	27
Chapter 4: Becoming a Parent	43
Chapter 5: Dad and Me	51
Chapter 6: On Turning Forty	65
Chapter 7: Divorce, Love and Becoming a Step-Mum	79
Chapter 8: Memories of Mum	91
Chapter 9: Becoming a Grandmother	105
Chapter 10: A Life-Changing Moment	121
Chapter 11: The Journey Continues...	133
Chapter 12: Of Lessons Learnt and Lessons Taught	139
Afterword	165
Acknowledgements	167
About the Author	169
Speaker Bio	171

Dedication

Mum and Dad, thank you for your love and guidance. You were always there, teaching me the values of life. I love you, thank you, miss you always, and will see you again someday.

Wendy, my sister and oldest friend. You germinated the seed of this book. Thank you for your love and support, for always being there and believing in me.

To my husband, Iain, thank you for your unwavering love and support in all things. You are my core, my strength and my soul mate.

My children and grandchildren, to whom I leave this book, now is your time to grow your own 'gardens.'

*'Cherish yesterday,
Dream tomorrow, Live for Today'*
- Richard Bach (author of Jonathon Livingston Seagull)

Introduction

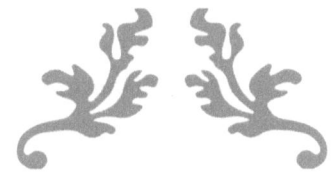

Many years ago, my mother wrote a journal called 'My First Fifty Years,' at the end of which she charged my sister and myself with continuing by writing our own stories.

This idea had laid dormant in my mind for many years until a remark by my sister during one of our many catchup calls. I had been telling her about my garden and how it gives me great pleasure to watch the seeds and seedlings I so carefully plant and nurture to grow and flourish. How working organically and learning all about living in harmony with nature has benefitted me. Her response was, "You should write a book!" I mulled this over in my mind and thought, 'Yes, I will do just that.'

At first, I thought my book would be about how I came to love gardening in just eighteen months because, you see, we had retired and decided to do the whole downsizing thing. We knew we wanted an old cottage, but more land and hubby had always wanted to live

Seasons of My Life

in the Midlands of Tasmania. A search on the internet soon had a shortlist of properties to look at. Within five minutes of walking into what would become our new home, we knew straight away that 'this was the one.' It called to us. A beautiful, quirky c1860 Victorian cottage on one acre with the start of a cottage garden and small orchard.

I knew I had a lot to learn about gardening, having never been much interested beforehand.

My love and passion for gardening developed, and I quickly realised my garden was teaching me so much about my life and soul.

Very quickly, my idea for what I would write about morphed as I realised I had a story to tell, a legacy to leave, and a vision of the world as I believed it should be. I began to realise that 'gardening' had always been a part of my life.

My parents had always encouraged and taught me authentic values; they enveloped me with love and provided a nurturing 'village' where I could thrive, remain true to myself, have faith in my abilities, and strive for greatness.

I have carried this on with my own children and now see them doing the same with my grandchildren.

Spring

A Time of Awakening

A time of awakening, your senses are new,
A canvas of possibilities, awaiting your view.
To flourish and grow, to see all and say hello,
The world extends its arms, ready to bestow.

An eager young bud has bloomed with grace,
Embracing the journey, at a steady pace.
Each petal unfurls, a story to tell,
A tale of resilience, where dreams can dwell.

Just look, dear soul, your future awaits,
A tapestry of moments, an intricate fate.
With boundless horizons, so vast and unknown,
You'll weave your own path, where passions are sown.

Chase your aspirations, let your spirit soar high,
Embrace the challenges, reach for the sky.
For within your being, a flame brightly burns,
A fire of potential, eager to learn.

The world is your oyster, a treasure to explore,
Seek out new landscapes, let your heart adore.
From mountaintop vistas to the ocean's embrace,
Each step taken forward reveals new space.

With open arms and an open mind,
May you discover wonders of every kind.
Embrace diversity, let compassion bloom,
And in the tapestry of life, leave your own unique zoom.

Seasons of My Life

A time of awakening, your senses aware,
The universe awaits, with infinite care.
So spread your wings, dear one, and take flight,
For your future is waiting, radiant and bright.

- Anne James

CHAPTER 1

Those Formative Years

It starts with Mum and Dad, now sadly passed. I 'see' them often in my garden, bending down to smell and pick a flower, pulling out a weed, touching a plant as they walk by, watching their great-grandchildren run and play; a tinge of sadness lingers as they never got to do this. I know they would have been so proud of their family, and this brings such joy and happiness now. Wonderful days of love and laughter, care and kindness. Mum is the organiser and Dad is the doer.

We were 'army brats' as Dad was a career soldier and led a nomadic life until he retired in 1972, when we settled into our permanent home here in Tasmania. Here I vividly recall days of Summer BBQs in the garden. Mum bringing out the salads to accompany the BBQ, fun under the sprinkler, and Dad tending his first veggie patch wearing his brown corduroy pants and burnt orange skivvy, sitting and happily digging and planting and weeding.

They were always gently but firmly tending their other 'garden,' raising my sister and myself to be strong and independent women. Rarely was a word said in anger, they would instead guide us to understand our strengths and learn from our mistakes. One of Dad's quotes that has stuck with me all these years is, 'Always strive to do and be your best. It does not matter what mark you receive. If you know you have done your best that is all that matters.'

Don't get me wrong, we were not perfect; nobody is. I was five years older than my sister and boy did she get on my nerves at times and there were the usual sibling spats. I was firmly but calmly reminded that as the 'big sister' I needed to look out for her. That we would eventually grow to be each other's oldest and dearest friends and champions, and that is exactly what we have become. My parents were always planting the seeds of our values and helping them to grow and flourish within us.

During our nomadic early years there are a few stand-out times that I often reflect on as they had very strong influences on the woman I would become.

The Avenue

14 Richards Avenue, Surry Hills, NSW

A passage from my mother's journal of her first fifty years best describes what 'The Avenue' was to our family.

Those Formative Years

'One of my aunts had a home in central Sydney and this home came to be known as "The Avenue" and was halfway house for all the family at some stage or another. My mother and I, and also Grandma lived here during the war years.'
- Elizabeth Marie Trevarthen

For me, this house became home for short periods as we moved from one home to another, one state to another, and even overseas for a three-year period. Such is the life of an 'army brat.' Mum, in later years, told me that I was an adaptable child and very nonplussed with all these changes. I think having very strong, loving and understanding parents gave me an appreciation of change. At the time all I remember is being very excited to see my grandma and great-aunts. They were fun, enfolded me into their home life, listened to me, told me stories and showed their love in a very Scots way. I spent so much time with them in my early years that I developed a slight Scots accent, something my school friends often teased me about, this did not much bother me as I was so proud of my family and even at a young age of my ancestry.

I have fond memories of sliding down the banister of the long staircase ('The Avenue' was a 3-story terraced house), going out to the laundry to help with stringing the doughnuts onto a broom handle when grandma and one of my great aunts were cooking them. Hiding behind great grandma's chair in the sitting room and hiding under the dining room table with its long tablecloth always on because it was my 'tent.' I would love sneaking the sugar cube bowl off the table to suck on the cubes, and yes, although I did get into trouble for this, it didn't stop me, and I am sure that bowl was positioned just in reach at times.

Seasons of My Life

During one of Dad's postings, we stayed at 'The Avenue' until an army home became available in Kingsgrove. I was only three at the time. Mum and Dad later asked me if I had any memory of that home and of an incident that happened one Sunday. And yes, I do have vague recollections of going on an adventure, which is not how Mum and Dad remember it!

> *'We became friendly with another young couple who had a daughter the same age as Anne. The two little ones played well together, and on this particular Sunday Anne had disappeared from our backyard. We assumed she had gone down to play with her little friend, and the other couple had thought the same of their daughter. Both girls were missing! Both fathers scoured the adjoining schoolyard with no trace of the little ones. Out came the cars to search the surrounding streets. Tony found them, on the busy Kingsgrove Road, at the traffic lights, sitting in the gutter. They each had little cases in their hands and were 'waiting for the light to change to go over where the lovely music was coming from' – the local church service was in progress. The ingenuity of three-year-olds, so how could we be very angry when it was a relief to see them safe and sound.'*
>   *- Elizabeth Marie Trevarthen*

It was also during this time at Kingsgrove that Mum and Dad took the opportunity of introducing me to the cinema and live music. I was taken to see 'The Sound of Music' not once but many times by Mum and Dad and also my great aunts. A movie that I have loved all my life and I confess have seen so many times I have lost count, not just for the beautiful story it tells but also because of the memories it brings forth.

Those Formative Years

Being taken to live entertainment and being exposed to shows and ballet also left me with a lifelong love of entertainment and astonishment at what ballet dancers are able to retell through movement.

Papua, New Guinea

I consider this one of the big adventures of my early childhood.

In preparation for the move to the province Papua, New Guinea in 1965, we moved back to 'The Avenue', and I remember that Dad travelled ahead, and we joined him some three months later.

In order to travel to another country, I had to undergo a schedule of vaccinations including TB and Smallpox. They hurt, but Mum told me I did this without a fuss or murmur. It must have been the preparation Mum undertook by explaining in simple language why I needed these, I was after all only four and a half at the time.

My main memory from that long plane journey was being bundled into warm clothes for the trip out of Sydney and then being changed into cooler clothing in the back of the plane for touch down in Darwin, and then onto Port Moresby. I vividly remember seeing Dad as he strode across the tarmac to greet us and have the memory of being enveloped in his arms, such a feeling of love and safety and warmth.

Dad was stationed at Taurama Barracks, and we first lived in a two-bedroom home on the hill overlooking the other homes, then moved into a three-bedroom home when my sister was born.

Seasons of My Life

Behind the back fence line was dense jungle and in our backyard were tropical fruit trees. I revelled in the taste of mango, pawpaw, banana and watermelon. My mouth and lips were always sore from the juice, and I remember the juice running deliciously down my arms. I can recall that fruit has never tasted as good as it did back then.

Life there was an adventure for me, hot and humid with two seasons, a lot of sunbaking, getting 'burnt to a crisp' and playing outdoors always under the watchful eyes of my parents or our houseboy, Philip.

Yes, we did have a houseboy, (male, domesic workers, who were often employed by military families), such were the times back then. However, Mum and Dad considered him 'one of the family' and helped him out whenever possible. You see, Philip was the main income earner for his family and was only nineteen years old when he came to us. He was devoted to us, and always wanted to *do* for us. In fact, Philip often shooed Mum away from household tasks saying, "No Missus, you no do." He and Mum would often have small arguments about who was going to do the cooking and laundry. Dad had often recounted tales of receiving his smalls from the laundry so stiff with starch that they 'stood up on their own!'

When my sister came along in 1966, Philip became her 'hero' and he doted on her as well as me. I remember him putting her into the laundry basket and dragging her up and down the hall to elicit squeals of excitement from her. He would also go out the back to pick fruit for us and then sit there and peel or open it for us to enjoy.

My bed was covered with mosquito netting, and I had to take malaria tablets. The air outside was also sprayed each evening and I remember having covers for over our food when the tank came down our street. I remember the 'chek, cheks' squeaking their way

Those Formative Years

down the glass of the windows and climbing up my wall at night, I loved those little geckos.

One thing I did not like very much were the big snakes, 'Black Paps' is what the locals called those big snakes, that would take the opportunity to curl up on the roofs of the homes. They were big, black and scary, and I thought one would come into my bedroom and swallow me whole.

I also picked up Pidgin English, (a mixture of English and local languages) very quickly and would, according to Mum, natter away quite happily with our houseboy. I think I must have considered him an uncle or older cousin. Never was I made to think of him in any other way by my parents.

In July 1966 Wendy was born, and I remember the first time I saw her, just staring at this tiny bundle and being so excited to have a sister at last.

A huge worry for my parents that I now understand, was that Wendy, unfortunately, became very prone to bronchitis and there was one time I remember well that she was struggling to breathe. Mum gathered her up in her arms to race next door for help. There was a slight dip in the ground, and she fell, dropping Wendy in the process. The shock of the fall got my sister breathing, but Mum twisted her ankle, and I ran screaming to our neighbours for help. All hands-on deck to look after them both and console me until Dad arrived from the barracks.

Another incident that occurred in early 1967 when I was six and Wendy was only six or seven months old, was one night when Mum and Dad had gone to a party or gathering. Our houseboy had gone home to visit his family and my parents organised for a local girl to babysit us. I have the memory of waking up because my sister was crying; she was still only a baby at this time. I went into her and then went looking for the babysitter, she was nowhere to be found. I remember feeling very scared, but I went back to my sister and patted her just like I had seen Mum do until she went back to sleep. I then remember just sitting at the loungeroom windows crying and waiting for Mum and Dad to come home and feeling such a huge sense of relief and no longer being scared when I saw them pull into the driveway.

As they later recounted, they were shocked to see me sitting there sobbing and calling out to them. They rushed in with Mum going in to check on my sister and Dad scooping me up in his safe, warm, and enveloping arms, hushing me and saying, "It's all right now," then taking me into Mum. Meanwhile, my sister continued to sleep blissfully through the whole thing.

It was here in New Guinea that I began my primary school education. Most of my memories are of having a lot of friends and enjoying playtime. It was so exciting being taken to school in the back of an army truck with an escort and then being picked up after school by a staff car to be taken to the barracks where I would be set up in Dad's office with pencil, paper and treats until Dad was ready to go home. Of course, Mum and Dad never let on that this was as a safety measure and that the escort vehicle was armed.

There were often parades at the end of each day and as Dad's office window looked over the parade ground, I would perch up on my chair, looking and listening as they played, bagpipes and all. I loved that music and watching the men march in step. I do truly believe it was here that my love of the haunting melody from bagpipes began and has, to this day, brought goose bumps to my skin and a feeling of warmth within me when I hear them being played.

Those Formative Years

Vietnam

This was a time in our lives that affected us all. I was ten when Dad left for his tour as 2IC (second in command) of 3RAR. It was very scary knowing I would not see him for a long time. In the lead-up to his going away, Mum and Dad kept their usual cool, calm selves going in front of us girls, but I now know as an adult how stressful this time must have been for them.

It was very exciting going down to see the ship Dad would leave on and saying, "Bon Voyage," but there were tears and long hugs as well.

Mum, her ever-resourceful and organised self, kept things as normal as possible at home. School, weekend activities, and holidays all continued. We would eagerly await letters and taped messages that came home from Dad on a regular basis. Mum would read out loud some of the letters and then would pause to read silently. Even as a young child, I knew they were private words of love, concern and care from Dad.

There were gatherings of all the Officer's wives and children often, and when tragedy struck for one of the wives it was impossible for Mum to hide this from us. You see her husband had been KIA (killed in action). Mum shielded my sister as much as possible as she was only very young, but she took me aside to explain what had happened; I remember being very upset. She took me in her arms and explained, "Yes this is awful, it is a risk soldiers take on, and we must care for his wife and help her through this time." Mum must have been very lonely and afraid during this time, but I do not remember her ever showing it. One stoic Scots woman there, she was, and it was something I inherited from her.

Seasons of My Life

During these two years 1970 and 1971, we were living in the foothills of Adelaide in married quarters, and I had developed close friendships quickly during this stay. Often on weekends when given my pocket money for the week I would walk down to the local store to buy some treats. From memory, a coke, bag of chips and bag of lollies cost me roughly the grand total of 20 cents! With a group of friends, I would also go on long walks along the tracks that led into the surrounding bush, with my lunch packed and a reminder to be home before sunset. There was no way for Mum being able to check up on me (no mobile phones back then) just a trust that I was sensible, responsible and knew what I was doing. I was given the freedom to have fun, *safe fun*, and able to explore my increasing independence.

At last, it was time for Dad to come home. I could not understand why we weren't going with Mum to see Dad arrive and why we could not stay with them that night but had to stay at home and be babysat.

"I don't need a babysitter, I am a big girl now," I had indignantly said.

"I know, but I need you to help the babysitter look after your sister," was Mum's very clever reply.

On the day of the welcome home parade, we were dressed in our best, knee-length boots and all, we headed into Adelaide to watch the parade from high up on a balcony in one of the buildings lining the street. Such excitement as Dad was spotted, he looked so handsome in his full uniform, I was jumping up and down until Mum put a gentle hand on my shoulder. There was much impatience as we waited for Dad afterwards, and boy do I remember those hugs!

Those Formative Years

I did notice that Dad was quieter on his return, something I would now recognise as reflection and even a certain amount of trauma. I do remember he would not talk about his time in Vietnam especially in front of us girls and it was not until I was much older that he did open up more to me about his experience there. I do vividly remember one thing he did say, "Thank goodness I have my family." Of course, I now know that this was in reference to the chemical warfare that was utilised and has caused so much grief for Veteran's and their families in the ensuing years, with a personal and lifechanging impact on Dad's health when he was forty-nine years old.

CHAPTER 2

A Place to Call Home

Shortly after returning from Vietnam, Dad was posted to Tasmania to take up a position as second senior officer in the state, which meant we were going home!

I was born in Hobart, Tasmania, and even though I had not lived in Tasmania except for a short period as an infant, it was always home to me. Mum and Dad always ensured we visited as often as possible during our nomadic years. Tasmania was also where both Mum and Dad were born and raised; Mum in Queenstown and Dad in Burnie, with Dad being local for all his youth and Mum for part of hers. Interestingly I found Dad's matriculation results on a Google search recently. He graduated in January 1951 and gained a Credit in Modern History and Higher Passes in English Literature, Economics and Geography.

Seasons of My Life

Tasmania was where my nan and pop lived (Dad's parents), where my only cousins were and where we would return each year, when able, for the Christmas and New Year periods.

Christmases at Nan and Pops were always a fun time, playing with my cousins, and chatting with Nan around the table in the kitchen; she was always interested in what I was doing and what I thought about various subjects, going on outings, Boxing Day where all the ladies and children would gather whilst the 'menfolk' went off to do their own thing. Going to the beach or pool, then back again for good old Tassie National Pies and/or ice-creams on the back lawn. Gobbling up sandwiches or toast with Nan's famous green tomato pickles or bowls full of home-grown raspberries and cream; so yummy I can still taste them.

Dad trying, in vain, to teach me how to ride a bike. I never succeeded as could not get a handle on how to balance and did indeed go over the handlebars a number of times! And despite trying many times over succeeding years, I never did get the hang of riding a bike. Trips to where my Pop worked, the local paper mill, with personally guided tours of the factory to learn all about paper making and its uses. Watching Pop tend his garden so full of veggies and flowers and so proud of his hydrangeas. He was a world of information and always had time to stop and listen to the natter of, and questions from a very curious granddaughter.

There was the time we were all piled into Pop's car on a trip out to Wynyard, I was sitting on Nan's knee in the front. No seat belt just her firm grip around me, we had stopped to pick up a bushel of peas that had fallen from the back of a truck, Pop had just taken off when another truck came past us at speed, throwing up a rock which hit the front windscreen and shattering it. Nan instinctively pulled me to her, covering my face as the glass fell in upon us. With no cuts, I was scared but excited, and Nan gathered a piece of the glass for me to keep. We all climbed out of the car so Pop could break out the rest of the windscreen and clear out the glass, then on we went with the wind whipping and blowing my hair around.

I remember on another trip; I must have been fourteen or fifteen at the time. All the adults were going to my aunt and uncle's place for the day. They had left my cousin and myself at Nan and Pop's as we wanted to do other things. With my cousin's friend, we decided to avail ourselves of the time to experiment with cigarette smoking and the drinking of Pop's whiskey! He had a large whiskey bottle in a dispensing cradle, and we would often watch as the adults partook of it in the evenings after dinner and wanted to 'know what all the fuss was about!'

Clever though, a brew of black tea was made to top up the bottle when we had finished, and the level of the whiskey marked. Oh boy, did I cough and splutter when first trying the whiskey and did not really like it but kept drinking to make myself look and feel all grown up. Did not take long until the effects of the alcohol and cigarettes took their toll and by the time Mum, Dad, Nan and Pop had returned I was feeling very 'green' indeed. Nothing was said at the time, I was just put to bed with nothing said the next day either. Instead, I was given an endless list of jobs to do to 'help out.'

In later years it was revealed to me that they all knew straight away what had been going on. Consent by all that my lesson had been learnt, not by chastisement but by how sick I felt the next day doing those jobs. It took all their efforts not to laugh or let on that they knew, and I have often done similar things with my own children, allowing them to learn by making mistakes and gaining the experience of life.

Seasons of My Life

It took many years for me to try whiskey again, I now love having a 'wee dram' on special occasions or 'just because I can', as does Iain. Single malt peated Islay Whiskey please! On a trip to Scotland in 2017 we consumed quite a bit and came back with seven bottles!

On arriving in Tasmania, we first went into army housing in one of the Northern Suburbs and enrolment organised in Primary School for both my sister and me. By this stage I was in my final year of Primary School and once again had to make a new set of friends. I made friends easily having been to six different schools in five years, including two separate schools whilst we were living in Papua, New Guinea.

The year 1973 saw me start high school, and all was going well in my new adventure. Then the announcement, Dad had resigned from the army after twenty-two years of dedicated service. His reasons for leaving were three-fold, as told by Mum:

> 'His next posting would undoubtedly be to Canberra where he would probably become insignificant unless he became a 'Yes man.' (A 'yes man' is someone who would agree or go along with others' plans, tasks or favours. Dad would not do this without checking in with his own values first. He would not blindly follow others.) This was never in his makeup. The second reason, Tony had lost the desire for further promotion, the gloss had worn off over the years. But I distinctly remember him saying it was my so-innocent remark three years earlier regarding the thankless task of unpacking which brought home to him the trials of upheaval we had all undergone.'
>   - Elizabeth Marie Trevarthen

And so began the hunt for the place we would all call *'home.'* Our very first home of our own! Mum and Dad included my sister and

A Place to Call Home

myself in this search. With us both being settled in our respective schools and with a strong network of friends they did not want to disrupt us, so the search was in the local area.

After quite a few house viewings I remember first seeing the place in Pascoe Avenue. Three-story weatherboard with a sandstone chimney, at the end of the Avenue. There was a big tree in the middle of the road and the gardens of the surrounding houses were so pretty. I was so excited and remember racing around the house soon claiming my bedroom. My sister did much the same, claiming the attic area as hers. Mum and Dad later told me that it was our enthusiasm that convinced them this was the home for us, and how right they were, I loved that place!

So many memories of home, family, celebrations, walking to and from school or being picked up by Dad (this was a real treat), birthday parties, my engagement, being married from this home and then returning there regularly when a parent myself for the short period of time that I was blessed with.

Sundays were always a time of coming together as a family around the table to discuss all that we had done during the week. Most times Mum would cook up a big roast with all the trimmings. The leftovers were saved for sandwiches for that night's tea. Dad would do the washing up afterwards with we girls 'swinging' on the tea towels. If one of us made the excuse, "I need to go to the toilet," their quick turnaround was, "You are doing an Aunty Joyce!" This in reference to one of my great-aunts who would invariably disappear when the clean-up happened.

Then Mum and Dad would settle into their armchairs to watch the TV, either a movie or during the footy season to watch the match being televised. Back then it was either a TFL (Tasmanian Football

Seasons of My Life

League) or VFL (Victorian Football League) match. Dad would usually fall asleep and snore! He never believed he snored so one time we took a picture and recorded his slumber. He was not amused when we told him what we had done but when he listened to the recording and eventually saw the photo, (we had to wait for it to come back from being developed, no instant sharing as now) he just laughed and said, "Okay, you have caught me out and I have to accept that I do snore."

Friends were always welcome in our home, always made to feel part of our family. Usually there was a BBQ involved or a different meal. With all our nomadic journeyings my sister and myself had been exposed to many cultures and cuisines. Dad did a particularly good 'back handed curry' or as he would put it, "Burns on the way out as well as on the way in!" We loved Asian, Italian, a bit of Greek and other European dishes. A family treat was to either go to a Chinese restaurant or have takeaways at home. Some of my friends had not really experienced these but they soon started asking what was for tea as they loved Mum's cooking too. This is something that I have enjoyed with my own family, I love to cook, have friends over and experiment with different recipes and different cuisines.

So, for me coming home entailed so much and continued my journey through life, falling in love for the first time, embracing change, making friends, and just beginning to grow my own 'village' all under the gentle guidance of my parents.

CHAPTER 3

Becoming a Nurse

Why did I become a nurse, a question that has been asked of me over the years. Simply it was to help people in need and who were sick.

Why did I not choose to become a doctor instead, another question often asked, because I wanted to be there 'hands on' at their bedside helping each day.

It did take me a while to also realise that nursing was not just something I did but was part of who I was and still am.

So, towards the end of my matriculation years, application was made, and interview undertaken to join the nursing school at a church run private hospital in Hobart. The year of starting was 1979 and in those days, nursing training was an apprenticeship, and you were indentured to the hospital. It also required that I 'board in' at the hospital, this was both exciting for me and a challenge as I had never lived away from home. I was required to stay in the nurses' home at the hospital for at least the first year of my training.

During my interview with Matron, I was drilled on the fact that I was already engaged to be married. I had to ask permission to be married and had to commit to not falling pregnant during my training! She sat so prim and proper behind her desk going through all the rules, regulations, uniform policy and protocols. At the end of the interview, she congratulated me on qualifying for entry to the nursing school, and I had to sign a contract. She then stood up, came around the desk to shake both mine and Mum's hands. A look passed between Mum and I and it was all we could do not to burst out laughing. Matron, so prim and upright in her uniform behind the desk, was wearing *slippers*! I knew then she was someone I could go to if ever I had an issue.

There was no university degree back then. It was straight in for a six-week school called Prep, then out onto the wards as a very young and naïve first year student. We were given all the mundane tasks like washing, bed changes, toileting, emptying bed pans and urinals, collecting false teeth for washing, wrapping bandages if there was a spare moment; it was very task oriented. Some of the patients would be very embarrassed by having a young female nurse tending to these jobs, so I would distract them by asking them about themselves and then listen whilst doing the task at hand. After all, this was part of caring for these patients, doing that which they were unable to, or struggled to do by themselves.

Becoming a Nurse

When time permitted, I would often go and pay a patient a visit towards the end of my shift, particularly if I had observed they had yet to have any visitors for the day. Asking them how they were, engaging and encouraging them to talk a little about themselves and their lives, and if there was anything else I could do for them—unconsciously building a rapport and trust, so important when managing a patients care.

I enjoyed my student years, they were hard, the study was intense through the various blocks taken over the three years. The shift work was challenging, always needing to be 'on the ball' and observing.

As each block of study was completed and I was back out on the wards, my duties became more complex, and by the time I was a third-year nurse, I was often placed in charge of the ward during nightshifts, overseeing more junior nurses and auxiliary nurses. Teaching what I had been taught and guiding them, I developed a philosophy of a 'See, Do, Teach' approach to teaching then and have carried this through my entire nursing career. My training involved external blocks of mental health, district nursing, midwifery (mainly in an observatory role.) There was also rotation into operating theatre and recovery, paediatrics and aged care.

Living in the nurses' home was fun and we became a close-knit community, each supporting one another in study and life. We went out together, met boyfriends or, in my case, fiancé, broke curfew and snuck back into the nurses' home, often just in time to shower and change for our shift the next morning. Oh, to have that energy now!

The building I was in had a fire escape just outside one of the other nurse's rooms, and there was a secret signal developed to let them know to leave the bedroom window unlatched so we could get back in. You see, each evening Deputy Matron would do a round at curfew to secure all windows and lock all external doors. I left the nurses home environment during my second year to return home in preparation for my wedding and moving to my first home with my husband. Exciting times and a bit of a struggle with managing work, study, arrangements for the wedding, finding a flat to rent. I could not have managed this without the loving support of my parents and partner.

I continued on through third year, intense study blocks, more senior roles on the ward, married life at home, final exams and then the nervous wait for results. All the nurses in my year were gathered together in the school for our results to be announced. As a whole we topped the state with overall results. I gained a distinction, I felt so proud of what I had achieved. My first year out was at the Repatriation Hospital looking after service men and women, veterans and their families. Some of the stories that were told are ones I cannot repeat for fear of being 'shot!'

It was during the 1980s that major changes began within the nursing profession in Australia. There was advocating for improved work conditions with a minimum of eight hours off between shifts, increase in rates of pay and shift penalty rates, and for nursing to be seen as a profession instead of an apprenticeship. Our unions were strong, and we were determined. With no progress the difficult decision to strike occurred in 1988. There was overwhelming support in the community but also detractors, as is always the case. At this time, I was on maternity leave, not directly involved, so I involved myself by supporting my fellow nurses by having discussions around the negative comments being made. All we wanted was to be recognised for the important role we played in patient care.

On one of my visits to my obstetrician, I arrived to a distinctly frosty air in reception. The reception staff were not talking to the obstetrician, and I soon found out why; he had made a comment that nurses were nothing more than 'glorified hand-maidens' and should stop all the fuss. Well, my back was up when I heard that, and when I went in for my appointment with him I did not hold back and gave him a piece of my mind. He was made aware very quickly that I was not amused, and I asked him to think about all that we did for his patients so that his visits to them went smoothly. We were there at the bed-side, caring for them, observing, trouble-shooting and alerting him at the first sign of problems, always ensuring the best care of his patients at all times, always managing multiple patients on any given shift. I also reminded him that we were living in the twentieth century and not in the eighteenth century! He saw the validity in my argument and apologised to me, to which I said, "You also need to apologise to all the nurses who so diligently care for your patients every day," and he did.

Doing home palliative care was very rewarding. I would go into my clients home for the overnight shift, giving the family of my clients some much needed respite of a full night's sleep by taking over the care required of their loved one, be it just sitting with the client, administering medication as needed, doing any dressings, helping them with personal care. Sometimes the client would not want me in the room with them and often the families would set me up in a nearby area, TV at hand, there would often be a cuppa ready on arrival. I would set up there and check in on my client at regular intervals. Stepping ever so quietly so as not to disturb them, or just gently speaking with them as I went about my duties. Being able to give this service brought so much joy and satisfaction and taught me so much more of all that is involved with nursing.

Moving back into acute care nursing in the early 1990s saw me working in accident and emergency, high dependency units and then intensive care. I was soon nursing patients requiring life support and critical care, caring not just for the patient but for their families too, who were very worried about their loved ones.

When a patient became well enough to transfer to the general ward, I would often wonder how they were faring. As ICU nurses we did tend to lose contact and would talk amongst ourselves about how they were doing.

One night when coming on shift, I was given a letter written by one of these patients I had cared for and looked after for four nights consecutively a few weeks prior. She was at that time still ventilated and under heavy sedation but was slowly 'waking up.' In the letter she thanked me for my care, for the calming voice that greeted her at the beginning of each night shift, orientating her to time of day and day of week, reassuring her each time I needed to rouse her to check on her level of consciousness or to tend to her. Then greeting her each morning with a cheery 'good morning.' At the end of this shift, I was then surprised by this person coming down to say hello to all of us that cared for her, and to put a face to the voice. It was moments just like these that made sometimes gruelling and challenging nights worth it all.

When I moved to General Practice nursing in 2009, I soon became interested and keen to develop my role to become that of a Chronic Disease Nurse, specialising in patient education and support, helping them to live well with their chronic conditions and not become defined by their various diagnoses. Here I was able to draw on all my experience thus far and apply it to my new role. I took on the responsibility to do courses on managing the various conditions from a nursing and patient perspective, applying active listening and compassionate guidance in goal setting.

Becoming a Nurse

I also became a mentor and preceptor for newer nurses coming into general practice and a mentor to medical students as they did their rotations. Always with that 'See, Do, Teach' approach. No question was ever *silly*, and I encouraged all to ask if they were not sure.

I had found my niche within nursing. I enjoyed working with the clients at the practice and had a wonderful, professional relationship with the doctors, other nurses and staff within this practice.

Over the years of my career, I have worked in a number of disciplines of nursing and the one take-away from all of my learning and experience is that I held true to those values 'gardened' by Mum and Dad and my wider 'village'. Nursing is so much more than tasks and duties, it is about purpose, care, compassion, tolerance and trust.

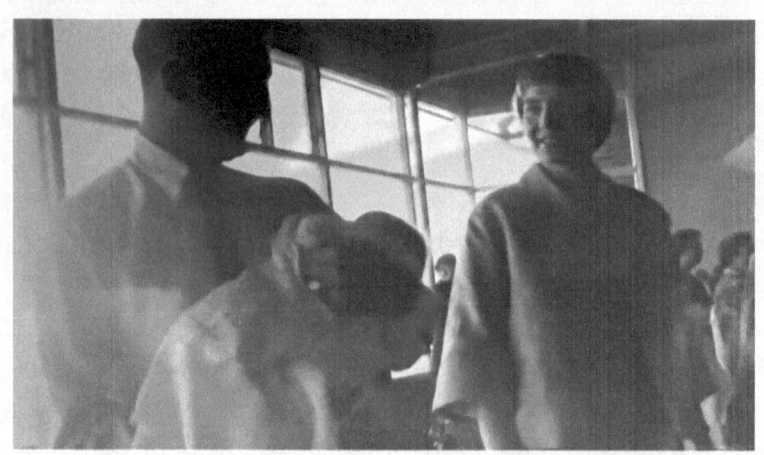

a. Top image, Dad meeting me for the first time.

b. Lower image, four generations of women, Lt to Rt: Mum, Great Grandma, Me, Grandma

a. Top image, Grandma and me, 1967.

b. Lower image, Wendy, Mum, Me (the legs) and Grandma, Ela Beach, 1967

a. Icecreams on the lawn at Nan and Pops (bottom left)

b. Mum, Wendy and Me. Listening to music sent home by Dad from Vietnam (top left)

c. Dad marching in Welcome Home Parade (top right)

d. Me all dressed up for Dad's Welcome Home parade (bottom right)

e. Battalion 2IC (Dad) sitting at his desk, 3RAR headquarters, Nui Dat, Vietnam, 1971

a. BBQ days, Pascoe Avenue

b. BBQ days, Pascoe Avenue

c. Dad tending his veggie patch, Pascoe Avenue

Summer

Summer's Promise

In the summer of my life, the tapestry unfurls,
Embracing passions, where dreams gently swirl.
Aspiration now dances, in sun-kissed skies above,
Guiding me with grace, like the peaceful dove.

Beneath the blazing sun, I bloom and grow,
The bud now flowered, eager for life to bestow.
The colours of experience, like a vibrant fire,
Ignite my soul and fuel my desire.

With each step I take, I shed my childhood shell,
Emerging as an adult, bidding innocence farewell.
The world before me, an open canvas so wide,
A palette of possibilities, where destinies collide.

In the depths of my heart, a tender seed has been sown,
Nurtured by time, a love so wholly grown.
Becoming a parent, a voyage filled with grace,
As love intertwines, a masterpiece takes place.

I witness life's miracle, in each innocent gaze,
A reflection of hope, a future that will never fade.
Through sleepless nights and lullabies sung,
I learn the power of love, the strength of the young.

In this summer of my life, hope finds its home,
A beacon of light, down which I will roam.
For in the embrace of passion, aspiration thrives,
Fuelling the fire within, where dreams come alive.

Seasons of My Life

And as the seasons change, and years gently pass,
I'll carry this summer's warmth, as life's looking glass.
For in the tapestry of memories, forever unfurled,
I'll find solace, love, and the essence of my world.

- Anne James

CHAPTER 4

Becoming a Parent

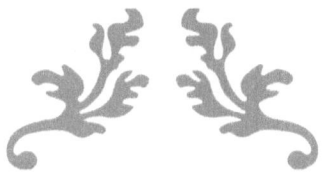

I had always wanted to be a mother and I instinctively knew I could raise my children in much the same manner as my parents did.

After marriage, my first husband and I made the decision to start a family together almost immediately, discussing the 'what ifs' and knowing we could manage what ever occurred.

A year later we were still trying, and then one day we found out the wonderful news. Just knowing I was pregnant filled me with such joy and a love so enveloping I could not wait to share the news with my parents and sister. Poor them, I could not wait until the next day, so late at night, my husband and I crept into my parents' home to tell them.

Seasons of My Life

My mother best describes the moment like this:

> 'It was around 11 o'clock at night, with Tony and I almost ready for sleep when we heard a key turn in the back door. Who should walk into our bedroom but Anne and her husband. They had smiles on their faces like Cheshire Cats, and both burst out with 'We're having a baby!' Then Wendy came running down the stairs to find out what all the commotion was about, and the squeals of delight were indescribable. Hugs, kisses and lots of laughter and chatter. It was wonderful news!'

I was fortunate that all was smooth sailing throughout the pregnancy, Mum and Dad were like a pair of 'mother hens' but never did they smother me or offer unsolicited advice. Their way of helping was practical; Dad getting the wood in when my husband was away, both having us over for meals, helping with setting up the nursery, and Mum knitting wonderful garments for the baby. All the while chatting away and only offering advice when asked.

As the forty-week mark approached, I became excited and impatient for this first child to make its way into our world. No, I did not know the gender as I wanted it to be a surprise.

Forty-one weeks, still pregnant and now waddling around like an elephant. I recall being in Hobart to do some last-minute nursery room shopping and running into a male acquaintance. He looked at me, looked at the size of my belly and tentatively asked when I was due. My reply was, "Last week."

The look on his face was priceless, and he urgently exclaimed, "What are you doing here in town, shouldn't you be home resting?"

My quick reply was to say, "I am pregnant, not sick."

Becoming a Parent

Our home was a half-way house for our extended family and friends, and we would often spend many enjoyable hours together, a meal always on the table and lots of laughter. I recall on the night before I went into hospital sitting quietly in my chair knitting and listening to all the conversation around me. Contractions had started and I was noting them down on a piece of paper. One of my male friends noticed I was pausing and jotting something down on a fairly regular basis. When he asked what I was doing, I calmly explained that I was in labour. You could have heard a penny drop for a moment and then there was surprise, shock and constellation as they all scrambled out of their chairs, wanting to know what I needed and what could they do. Let me explain, we were one of the first couples in our group of friends to have a child, so everyone was very anxious for us. I burst out laughing and gently told them, "Don't fuss, it's only labour and I have a long way to go before I deliver." Such was the care present in the 'village' we had become part of.

My daughter, Danielle, born the 21st of April 1983, deciding she was too comfortable inside me, was slow to present herself to the world and so began the process of moving the labour along. Boy did I know all about it then! Just before she made her appearance we could hear a cannon salute and bells ringing in the distance. It was not until a short while after my delivery that Mum and I realised why. My daughter shared a birthdate with Queen Elizabeth II, and we had been able to faintly hear the twenty-one-gun salute coming from Anglesea Barracks in the city. I have often joked with Danielle that the salute was in fact, 'in honour' of her finally arriving!

My mother and husband were with me throughout the labour, and again my mother wrote about this in her Journal:

> 'And we all patiently waited through the next few months for Anne's confinement. Then the day arrived, I felt honoured

yet humbled to be allowed to witness Anne's labour, to wipe her brow, to slip chipped ice into her mouth and to hold her hand through each contraction as they became stronger and stronger. The moment of birth was a wonderous experience for me as their beautiful daughter came into the world. Oh! Tony and Wendy were soon on the scene to see this new member of our family. This is an experience I will never forget.'

Holding my daughter for the first time, words are hard to find, the love that washed over me was like nothing I had ever experienced before. I laughed, I cried, I could not take my eyes off her and was so reluctant to hand her back to the nurses. I wondered who she would be and what she would become. I pledged to my daughter that I would always be the best mother I could be, love her, nurture her and guide her through to womanhood, just as I had been by my parents.

This beautiful girl became a happy, curious child, keen to learn more about her world and loved nothing more than playing with us, being read to and then tentatively learning to read herself with our guidance. In fact, by the time Danielle started school she could already read and write quite well for her age. Her preschool teacher was a bit dubious about me very proudly telling her this, so I asked her to fetch any book off her shelf and pick out any paragraph. With the book handed to Danielle, she so proudly read it out loud. Any challenging words sounded out just as we had taught her. Danielle did well at school, was quite academic and fairly early on decided she wanted to either look after other children or become a teacher. And teacher, she did in fact become, even being both mother and teacher in the classroom to both her children.

Five and a half years later, I was pregnant again with our second child. Again, a trouble-free pregnancy, this time however I was

Becoming a Parent

unable to have my mother present during my labour and delivery because by this time my dad was ill, having contracted Guillain-Barre Syndrome when my daughter was five-months old. He was home with Mum but paralysed from the shoulders down, so totally reliant on Mum for pretty much everything.

When I went into labour, we stopped at Mum and Dad's house on the way to the hospital, to reassure them all was okay. Dad's words were, "What are you doing here, get yourself to hospital. I love you."

And so, Luke Anthony, born the 27th August 1988, our beautiful boy came into the world, again that all-enveloping love was immediate.

Silly me, on the night after his birth he was sleeping in his cot beside me, I was watching a movie about two mothers whose babies were accidently swapped at birth in hospital. Well, I scooped him out of the cot, crying and holding him close. That was not going to happen to me, no way, no one was going to take him out of the room. The nurses found me this way when they came in to check. They understood, calmed me and reassured me – the 'mumma bear' was out for all to see!

On our way home from hospital some four days later we again stopped in to see Mum and Dad. Mum had been able to visit us for a short time in hospital to meet her first grandson and to be able to reassure Dad that all was okay. This visit was to allow Dad to meet his grandson for the first time. I laid my infant son down on Dad's chest and helped him put his arms over his grandson. Wonderful tears of joy streamed down his face, and I still hear to this day his soft words of greeting to his infant grandson, "You beautiful boy, oh how I wish I were able to take you to football, cricket and teach you how to golf. I will just have to tell you all about it when you are older, and we can lie here and watch all the sport together." As Luke grew up, he did develop a love of sport and did indeed take up football, cricket and golf. Dad would have been so proud.

My boy, the adventurer and risk taker, it was about four years later, a beautiful weekend day and the children of our neighbourhood were out in the street (it was a quiet cul-de-sac) enjoying themselves, riding their bikes, playing street cricket, all the while being watched over by all the adults. Danielle had a friend over and they and Luke were out on the sidewalk drawing using board chalk. The mother of Danielle's friend had arrived to pick up her daughter. We had stood out talking for a while and then I had gone back up inside for some reason. Suddenly, I heard screaming and everyone yelling out to me to come quickly. As I made my way out, I saw, to my horror, my son lying under the belly of their four-wheel drive, not moving. He had crept backwards under the front of it to make way for more drawing on the pavement and no one saw him do this. My heart went into my mouth and as I saw Danielle trying to pull him out, I yelled out to not move him. He did then start to move himself, out from under the car and then collapsing to the ground.

I do not remember getting down to him but was later told I raced down the stairs so fast it did not seem like I was touching them. I slid under him to hold him still, yelled out for an ambulance to be called and to fetch a towel to wrap around his neck to hold it still. All the while I was talking quietly to him to keep him calm. Ambulance arrived along with the police, and I don't remember much about the trip to hospital with him.

Many examinations and tests later, his only injury was a twist fracture of his lower leg, thank goodness. Plaster on, paediatrician called for review and admission with me staying by his side all the while. After two days in hospital, I insisted Luke be reviewed for

Becoming a Parent

home care. Indignantly I was told by a Registrar that discharge was not viable until they were sure he could manage crutches as he could not possibly be carried around by me. My indignant reply was, "I carried him for nine months and I will carry him for the rest of my life if necessary." So, home we went with the blessing of his paediatrician. Again, the 'mumma bear' had come out.

Although five years apart in age, my children were close. Danielle was, for the most part, very patient with Luke; she would play with him, read to him. They were normal children, would do things they knew they should not, as parents we were learning as we raised them, it took a lot of patience, and yes, like all parents we would become frustrated at times.

I remember one episode with Danielle, she must have been only three or so at the time. We were at a department store and as many children do, she saw something she wanted. Of course, when I said 'no' there was the big melt down. Or as I like to call it, a 'kitchen floor reset.' Well, 'no' meant 'no' in our family, so I just stepped over her and pretended to walk off, she soon stopped, got up and ran after me.

Another time she had her father and I in stitches when she so innocently said whilst watching Play School one morning and the presenters were doing the 'What's in the Box' segment, "I know, I know...it's a turd!"

"What?" we said between bouts of laughter.

"You know...that thing...like a frog."

Then there was the time Luke so innocently asked his father if the dinosaurs were around when he was little. This was when we were going over to see my in-laws. Luke at this stage was very fascinated in dinosaurs and had been asking if the bridge we were passing over had been there then!

There were the usual sibling squabbles but mostly Danielle and Luke were close. That relationship has not changed, and they remain very close to this day. They may not talk all that often as they lead busy lives raising their own children and working hard, but family times together are always special and precious. They each raise their own children with love and care, and I watch on proudly as I see them planting and nurturing their own values within their children.

Parenthood was all that I thought it would be, the ups and downs, teaching, guiding and watching them grow, go to school, make their career choices, love, heartbreak, love again, marriage, and now children of their own. So gently and mindfully tending my 'garden' and teaching them the values by which they live today. They too, now have their own 'village' around them, guiding, and supporting each other.

During the writing of this book, we celebrated my daughter's fortieth birthday, boy do I feel old! What a Wonderful day and during a quiet moment in the afternoon, I took pen to paper and wrote:

> *As I sit here this afternoon having a wee quiet moment, I reflect on this day celebrating Danielle's fortieth birthday! Surrounded by family and friends, the table groaning with food for all. Enough dessert to feed an army. Music, laughter, good cheer and the next generation all running around, playing so well together. The entire 'village' looking over them, keeping them safe but allowing them the freedom to make their own fun and enjoy themselves. In my mind's eye I see those no longer with us, but so present in spirit. I only need to gaze at my own children to see them reflected.*

CHAPTER 5

Dad and Me

Anthony Rex Trevarthen
B 1933 – D 1991

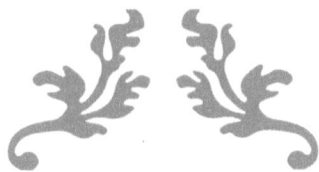

Dad, my hero, my rock and confidante, he was gentle, caring, a loving husband, father and grandpa and not afraid to show his emotions as so many men of his generation were.

He was often described by his friends and colleagues as 'a gentleman's gentleman.' Having two girls, he would always describe himself jokingly as 'being in a petticoat government.'

Discipline for him was to discuss the issues and arrive at a solution together. Don't get me wrong, we always knew when we had done wrong or taken a misguided step, however there was never an instant of a voice or hand raised in anger. In fact, the only time I remember raised voices from either of my parents was one evening before he went to Vietnam. Mum and Dad had come back from an evening gathering, I was asleep in the bedroom and awoke to raised voices and what was obviously an argument taking place between them in the loungeroom. I wandered out crying and immediately they stopped. Dad carried me back to my bed; they sat down together and apologised for upsetting me. The content of the argument was not discussed, instead they looked at each other, held hands, kissed and apologised to each other and then went on to teach me that I should never go to sleep on an argument. That it was okay to have a difference of opinion, and to respect each other's opinions.

Of course, as an adult and thinking back on this incident, I understand that the worry and anxiety around Dad's impending departure for Vietnam was weighing heavily on their minds. I have no distressing thoughts about this memory, I look back on this as yet another way in which they taught me my core values.

When Dad made the decision to resign from the army in his early forties, Mum became the main bread winner for our family. Dad searched for a job but came up against barriers due to his age! He did share his concerns, as by now I was pretty clued in to how this could affect him. He eventually found positions with the local RSL, Tasmanian Umpires Association and Rifle Association, and our dining room doubled as an office.

He had more time now to spend with 'his girls', supporting us in all our school, social and, for my sister, sporting endeavours. I was not much interested in sports, being more interested in arts, sciences and very keen on music.

Dad and Me

There had always been music in my life, and both my parents encouraged my interest in music. I grew up listening to the music of my parents' era; classical, pop, rock, jive, band, dance music, you name it and would love to watch as Mum and Dad would dance to some of their favourite tunes. In fact, I still have some of their LP's (long play).

In high school I took up flute, 12-string guitar, and even dabbled with the cello. I participated in school orchestra, solo performances, a folk guitar group, doing medieval madrigals of all things.

As an adult I surrounded my children with music, of listening, singing along, dancing to and encouraging them to include music in their own lives. They do this to today, each with their own personal tastes on musical genres but an appreciation for all music.

Seasons of My Life

Music in Life

Nature's orchestra, is a soulful refrain,
To every season, a delight to contain.
The vibrant song of birds, a joyful thrill,
While bees hum melodies, their purpose fulfilled.

Leaves flutter down in a gentle ballet,
Their rustling whispers, a melodic display.
Raindrops that dance, to thunder's roar,
As wind whispers secrets through branches galore.

In silence too, a symphony is found,
A stillness that stirs, not a single sound.
Closing my eyes, I let the melodies play,
And they wash over me, in a mystical array.

So often loud, calling forth passion's fire,
And then it is soft, a lullaby sung by mother.
Music breathes life into every moment we live,
And in turn, life breathes music, a precious gift to give.

With emotive grace, it touches my soul,
Igniting emotions that only music can console.
In cadence and rhythm, my heart finds release,
A symphony of existence, bringing me peace.

The notes guide me, like a gentle breeze,
Through life's winding paths, amidst hills and seas.
Embrace the symphony, both fierce and serene,
For the music in life will always be.

- Anne James

Dad and Me

Time moved on, and I was now in my final year of matriculation, which we now call college, I had met the boy who would become my first husband and one evening over the phone of all things, he proposed to me.

There was an upcoming family holiday to the east coast of Tasmania to a favourite spot, so we waited until then before saying anything to the family. Nervously, and in the old-fashioned way, my fiancé stood up and asked permission for my hand in marriage, we were not quite eighteen at this stage. No questions about, were we too young? Were we sure, or shouldn't we wait until we were a bit older? Dad just got up with a huge smile on his face, shook my fiancés' hand and said, "Of course." That was closely followed by hugs, kisses and the opening of a bottle of 'bubbles' to celebrate.

On the day of my wedding some two years later, I had some very special and private moments with Dad as we got into the car, arriving at the church and then him firmly but gently patting my hand as we walked down the aisle for him to 'give me away'. My wedding was very traditional, but I would not have it any other way, there was a very strong Scottish heritage within my family, and I wanted to pay homage to this.

1983, the year of my daughters' birth and the year of a huge change in all our lives. One day in September I received a call from Mum, she was very distressed and asked me to come quickly.

I will now let Mum describe that time in her own words:

> 'On the morning of the 28th of September 1983, Tony complained of feeling unwell and quite weak, so much that he felt I should drive him to the doctor's surgery. The diagnosis

was the probable onset of gastroenteritis and antibiotics were prescribed, and Tony duly went to work.

That evening, Tony surprised me by saying at 8:30 PM, he was going to bed. I recollect watching him walk through the kitchen towards the hallway and I made the remark that he seemed to be waddling like a duck, rather than walking in his usual upright fashion. Tony's retort was, "Don't be stupid, woman!"

During the night I was aware of a sweet aroma emanating from Tony, not his usual male scent, later, much later, in discussions with family and medical staff, I mentioned the aroma, but no significance seemed to be attached to it. But I have my own theory about this phenomenon.

Imagine my surprise to be woken at 6:30 AM the next morning, the 29th of September, by Tony standing at the bedroom door, supporting himself with arms outstretched, saying, "I have no power in my hands, I can't even flush the toilet!"

I told Tony to go back to bed and I would contact his doctor. Again, I saw this duck-like walk, but made no mention of it to Tony for fear of upsetting him.

His doctor was very prompt in answering my request for him to make a home visit so early in the morning. In his usual brusque manner, he told us that Tony had not had a stroke, but there was the possibility of pneumonia. Another prescription was written for further antibiotics, and I hurried to the pharmacy to have this made up. By the time I had returned Tony had become quite agitated and anxious to begin the medication.

Dad and Me

Tony scarcely had the strength to hold a glass of water, so I assisted him to take his tablet.

The day wore on through until just after lunch when I, too, became anxious for Tony's welfare. His speech had started to slur, and his arms were just lying there, not moving. In my anxiety, I contacted our oldest daughter, Anne, who was a trained nurse. She arrived quite quickly, went straight to her father, and asked him to push down with his legs onto her hand. He couldn't. She tried the same with his hands, and again he couldn't.

Anne and I moved to the family room where we quietly talked about what should be done. Anne's advice was of two options, another doctor's opinion or call an ambulance, with her strongly opting for the ambulance. This we did.

It was mid-afternoon when Tony was transferred from our bedroom into the ambulance. Anne remained at our home to wait for her sister, Wendy, to arrive from college. I, of course, travelled in the ambulance with Tony.

Halfway down our street I saw Wendy walking towards us and asked if we could stop so that we could let her know what was happening. Wendy was devastated to see her father in the back of the ambulance, and I told her to go home to Anne who would explain things to her.

The ambulance arrived at the emergency department of the public hospital at approximately 4:00 PM. Here Tony was assessed repeatedly by several different doctors using sensation testing apparatus on the soles of his feet with no response. I could see that Tony was becoming more and more agitated with fear beginning to show in his eyes. Eventually a resident doctor from the intensive care unit came to assess Tony, and after his examination advised us that Tony had Gillian Barre syndrome. At last, a definitive diagnosis, but what was it? We were to learn a lot about this syndrome as time went on.

Eventually Tony was transferred into ICU, but I had to wait, for what seemed an eternity, before I was allowed to see him in this ward. The time is etched in my mind, 6:30 PM, when an ICU Sister called me through, and my first concern was Tony's eyes. They were red rimmed and bloodshot. My first words to him were, "Oh! Darling, what have they done with your eyes."

Initially I took no heed of the drip lines into his body the tube up his nose or the other pieces of ICU paraphernalia surrounding his bed. All I was seeing were his poor eyes still filled with fear.

Soon afterwards, Anne and Wendy arrived and were told what had happened to their father. We could see that Tony was becoming very tired, so we agreed, reluctantly, to leave him in the capable hands of the staff of ICU and allow him to have some rest.

Anne was my strength that night, taking it upon herself to advise Nan and Pop, Tony's parents in Burnie, of Tony's hospitalisation. I recall her stressing that he was not going to die, but he was seriously ill and that I would keep them informed.

This was the beginning of a long, arduous time ahead for all of us.
- Elizabeth Marie Trevarthen

Dad and Me

And so, the long journey began for all of us, Dad's condition was tenuous, on full life support, susceptible to infections which could so easily take his life. Trying to maintain our daily lives and ensuring that wherever possible at least one of us was with Dad. I would go in the evenings to read to him, talk about the day. At first, I was unable to tell if he was able to take all this in, but I knew how important it was to keep him connected with the family and the world around him.

There was always a radio on during 'waking hours' in his ICU room. Then, suddenly eye movement was noticed under his eyelids. The Caulfield and Melbourne Cup days were coming up, Dad loved his horse racing, so the ICU staff moved their TV into Dad's room and Mum held his eyelids open. Huge elation and quite a few tears came from everyone as we watched Dad move his eyes. This was progress.

Knowing by speaking with Dad's doctors and doing my own research to help us all understand his illness, was that he would probably not make a full recovery. This news did not deter any of us. At each visit we would encourage Dad to 'hang in there' and keep fighting. This is something I would also repeat to myself like a mantra to help me get through each day.

I recognised how important it was for me to keep up my own strength mentally and was very aware how all this was affecting my family. So, we all agreed that it was important to each have some time off to rest and recharge.

During all this time, in total Dad spent around three years in hospital and rehab there were some stand out moments. The time he started to show movement, firstly in his jaw, then tiny finger movements, being able to wiggle his torso in the bed, able to hold his eyes open independently thus allowing us to communicate using an alphabet board. Then Dad surprising Mum one day by being able to hold his arms up long enough so that he could give her a hug. When my daughter saw this, she then insisted that she get a hug from 'Papa' at each visit.

As Dad's strength improved, he was gradually conditioned to being able to recline in a wheelchair and so with ICU staff, ventilator and other equipment in tow would be taken on walks around the hospital, out into the streets and eventually on short day visits home to Mum.

When my sister's eighteenth birthday approached, Dad was worried he would miss the celebration, however Mum and the ICU staff had other ideas. It was organised that he would attend with a paramedic, two ICU nurses and all the paraphernalia required. On arrival at the venue, it was all hands on deck from family and friends to get him out of the ambulance and into the venue. What a most marvellous evening with everyone popping over to Dad to say *hello*, and him being able to see his daughter celebrate her birthday.

On the 27th of October 1984 Dad was able to be taken off the ventilator. In the lead up to this momentous occasion one of the ICU nurses, Les Valentine, created a motivation chart for Dad's wall. It was a countdown graph showing the ventilator at the beginning and then at the end of the ventilator being thrown into the rubbish bin, such was the care and compassion of those wonderful nurses throughout Dad's ICU stay. Such an achievement and as Dad's respiratory muscles got stronger a slow wean of tracheostomy tube to one that allowed him to speak. To hear his voice after so many months still brings tears to my eyes.

July 1985 – the day of my sister's wedding. She was now living on the mainland, and we all missed her so much. It was organised for

Dad and Me

Dad to come home for the day. By this time Mum and I were able to do all that was necessary for Dad's care. We were all excited, but also sad for the fact that none of us could be there. A time for a phone call from Wendy shortly after the wedding had been arranged, and it was just before this happened that Dad voiced his frustration and sadness at what had been taken from him.

"It isn't fair," he said. And it was those words that summed up exactly how we were all feeling. A bottle of bubbles was on standby, and it was at this moment that we heard the cork being popped by my then husband. So, glasses were raised to celebrate amidst tears and laughter.

Time moved on and Dad eventually was able to come home permanently. It was a momentous day! This was again a time of change and there were times when I would visit that it fell to me to support both my parents emotionally as they adjusted to their new lives together. Their love for each other and their strength of purpose was amazing to witness.

My children never knew their grandfather any other way, he was just Grandpa to them, and they loved visiting and chatting with him. Mum and Dad would often arrange for small treats to be ready for any visit, and Danielle and Luke loved looking under Dad's hands for their chocolate frogs. Danielle would help out when there, turning the pages of the newspaper for Dad, helping Mum with his personal care, such as feeding him, giving him drinks. Luke would try too but being a toddler, he struggled with some of the tasks; food and drink would easily be spilt, and Dad would laugh and hug them in his own way. He loved spending time with them, and they loved climbing up onto the bed to be close with him. He was always keenly interested in what they were doing and made a very big deal out of any drawings or letters they wrote. Of course,

Luke's were scribbles being so young, this did not matter. They were all proudly displayed in the bedroom where Dad could see them.

So that Dad was included in all family events we held children's birthday celebrations there, Christmas traditions continued. When it came time for Mum's birthday or Mother's Day she was always charged with, "Give Anne the money for lunch and an amount extra." He would then instruct me on what gift I should get from him to her.

Then in mid 1991 Dad became very ill with pneumonia and was readmitted to hospital. He'd had one previous six-week stint in hospital when I was pregnant with my son, this requiring ventilation for a brief period. And it was during this time that he made the decision that he wanted no more interventions but just to be made comfortable for any future events.

His wishes were respected. He slowly deteriorated, and at around midday on the 27th of June 1991 he peacefully passed away. The 1st of July 1991 was the day of Dad's funeral.

My memories of this day are like a kaleidoscope of emotions, thoughts, sounds and images.

On waking up that morning to the sound of sobbing, realising it was my own. Crying for the loss of Dad, crying for me in my grief. I then did what I often do, pulled myself together, set my emotions to one side for the moment so I could gather my strength. For myself, for my mother, for my sister, and for my children. Arriving for the service, such a large congregation had gathered, of family, friends, colleagues, all there to support us and to show their profound respect for Dad.

Dad and Me

The image of my son, just shy of three, wearing his suit with his Grandpa's medals proudly pinned to the right side of his jacket. Of my daughter, a tender eight years old, needing comfort, but offering comfort also. Dad's favourite song 'Ave Maria' being played. Then at the crematorium, his 'Poppy Service', a service conducted by the RSL for ex-service personnel. Seeing Dad's coffin draped in the Australian Flag. The poppies laid on his coffin. The 'Ode of Remembrance' being recited.

One Minutes silence observed by all.

Then the *'Last Post'* echoing from the back of the room.

They shall not grow old as we that are left grow old
Age shall not weary them, nor the years condemn
At the going down of the sun and in the morning
We will remember them
- The Ode from Laurence Binyon's Poem,
For the Fallen, (1914)

Lest we Forget

CHAPTER 6

On Turning Forty

The start of the new millennium and my fortieth, the year 2000.

There had been lots of discussions and differing opinions on when the new millennium would begin, and who could forget the whole Y2K Millennium bug issue that seemed to capture the world's attention with various theories of what would happen, with many feeling it was 'the end of the world.' Within my own 'village' there were many interesting and challenging discussions and theories around all of this. I personally paid it minimal attention as I have never prescribed to scaremongering, my parents had always encouraged me to do my own research, ponder and look for the truth of the matter, then make up my own mind.

Seasons of My Life

And then, on the 1st of January 2000, we all woke up. No planes fell out of the sky, no computers crashed, and the world was still there, just as it had been the day before.

I reflected on how far we had come since I was first introduced to the world of computers in high school in 1976. From memory, it was one of the PCPs with a large standing metal storage box holding the disk storage units, in a booth around 2x2 metres. We would be sat at a desk with keyboard and screen and were introduced to BASIC language (Beginner's All-purpose Symbolic Instruction Code).

The World Wide Web was then made a public domain in the early 1990's and our first home computer was a Commodore 64! You could key in a search, go away, cook dinner, take a walk then come back to check on the progress of the search. Would sometime take hours and I vividly remember the noise they made! This computer was affectionately dubbed the 'great timewaster!' Look how far we have come to today.

And then there was the 'text messaging' of my teens and twenties. I was rummaging through one of my memory boxes and came across two examples of this: short, handwritten notes, one from my sister and one from a high school friend.

Dear Anne,
Thank-you for offering to make the clothes that I want out of the style book. I hope you do get married (and have 2 kids). When I am in the same situation that you are in now, you'd be the first one to know, I promise. Thank-you for being a wonderful sister and a 'punch around friend.'
Love and best wishes,
From Me (Wendy, Taxi)

On Turning Forty

Dear Anne,
Well just a short letter of thanks. Just knowing you have someone to lean on anytime is a very reassuring thought. All turned out well on Sunday, keep your fingers crossed! I just hope that you realise you can lean on me anytime also.
Bye for now,
Your friend for now and always. XXX (name withheld)

I had also lived through the introduction of mobile phones. From the first one coming to Australia in the early 1980s being an exorbitantly priced handset, weighing in at 14kg, the receiver needing to be stored in the boot of your car with antenna on the roof. Memory was very limited to only *sixteen* numbers—such a status symbol and only for the very affluent, which was not us.

It was not until hand-held devices became readily available and affordable that we got our first one, sometime in the early 1990s. Still very cumbersome and described as a brick, analogue, heavy, lots of background noise and static. No text messaging, no camera, no video.

Just look at this technology now. From sitting in a computer room at school to now having a mobile phone in my back pocket. Instant and constant connection with family and friends, social media, and the internet at my fingertips. I now carry a telephone, computer, camera and video around. I even watch TV and stream movies in one simple device.

Who knew! Science fiction (remember those scenes in the original Star Trek series?) turned into Science Fact in thirty-two short years.

July 1969! To have borne witness to 'Man's Landing on the Moon' was something I still, to this day, find amazing.

Seasons of My Life

At the time my family were living in Point Lonsdale, Victoria, and I was attending Point Lonsdale Primary School. When I close my eyes I can so easily picture that time. Mum had woken me early in the morning to say they had landed. I remember squealing with a child's delight even though at eight I probably did not fully understand the true significance of this event.

It was a Monday morning and school beckoned for me. Mum and Wendy went to a neighbour's house to watch. Dad would have been at work at Queenscliff Barracks.

I remember lining up with my classmates and marching to the hall where we all sat on the mats to gaze up at a somewhat puny TV screen. When those first grainy pictures were broadcast, I just sat there in childlike wonder at what I saw and heard. It was just like something out of a movie. I know we sat there until the end of the school day just watching and listening and when I got home from school and Dad got home from work, we all sat around our TV to watch the news broadcast. Mum and Dad kept looking at one another and shaking their heads in amazement at what the world had witnessed that day.

Embracing the change and adapting to it, incorporating it into every aspect of our lives. I found this exciting and challenging, and understood that my own children would grow up in a world of ever evolving AI. So, for me it was important to encourage them to embrace what they had at their fingertips but also to encourage them to see the real world and remain a part of that too.

Part of that shift was to embrace more fully the 'village' I had around me, of elders, family and friends and as my children grew, their

On Turning Forty

friends. My children were encouraged to begin to find their own way and it had been such a joy to watch them as they spread their wings and began to become more independent. There had been sadness and loss and they understood this was part of life, we as a family were open and discussion was always encouraged. There had also been wonder, achievement and the beginnings of working towards their own goals and ambitions.

Family and friend gatherings were frequent and there were many wonderful times together. Close friends were like aunts and uncles to my children and to this day they still call them aunt or uncle, demonstrating the closeness, inclusivity, and importance of their 'village'. And then there were the special moments and gatherings...

Christmas Eve had always been the gathering time for friends at our home. Lots of food, laughter, catching up, swapping of stories, then 'The Night before Christmas' read to the children, Carols by candlelight on the television, and a tradition that is still carried through to today even if not physically together, of standing and singing along, at the top of our voices, to the 'Hallelujah Chorus' from Handel's Messiah. I always get a text message during this, of 'hellalujahhhhhhhh!' With emojis of champagne glasses, party faces, love hearts.

Christmas Day: The tradition in my father's family and the one that I grew up with is of excitedly waking up on the morning to a small present from 'Santa' at the foot of my bed, seeing all the presents under the tree but having to wait until the gathering of Nan and Pop's friends for morning tea. Then with parents, grandparents, aunts, uncles and cousins we would gather around the tree. Usually Pop would be 'Santa' as each present was given out and we would wait for the person to open it to the 'oohs' and 'ahhs' of all around.

Seasons of My Life

Mum and Dad would pop small cryptic clues on mine and my sisters presents, a tradition I have carried on to this day.

New Year's Eve: a quiet one for us now, however, during my younger adult years always a gathering at our place, again lots of food and drink, laughter, and fun. The children staying up as they got older but when younger going to bed and always there would be one of the adults checking in on them regularly.

Then the home dinner parties shared between two other couples with young children. Each taking it in turn to host throughout the year. At one such in my home it was decided that I would prepare the meal (always a three course and different cuisines) ahead of time. A screen was placed to block the kitchen from view, my friends were told the children were at their grandparent's place and a chef had been hired for the evening. Distinct music of the Swedish chef from Sesame Street was playing and who should walk out with the first course, but my children dressed as the chef. So much laughter at this.

As my fortieth birthday approached it was decided to have two celebrations, you see my then husband was also celebrating his fortieth just two days from mine. With a very large group of family and friends it was decided to hold two celebrations just to fit everyone in. One for extended family and one for immediate family and friends. All helped out and what wonderful celebrations they were. It was so wonderful having everyone around me, helping me celebrate.

I remember reflecting on when my own parents turned forty, how old I thought they were and now here I was turning forty and not feeling old at all. How our perspective changes as we grow wiser. One thing I have always said since I turned forty and asked

On Turning Forty

how old I was, "I am twenty-one again with some many years of experience." So at forty, I was 'twenty-one again with nineteen years of experience.' I am now approaching my sixty-third birthday and do not feel old at all, in fact I will be twenty-one again with forty-two years of experience! I firmly believe in staying young at heart and in mind. That life experience helps shape you as a person, your beliefs and values do evolve over time. Mistakes and detours along the way happen, as long as you learn from these. Remaining true to yourself and your values, surrounding yourself with a 'village', teaching, nurturing and guiding your children as they grow. Having purpose and passion in your life, embracing the funny and enjoying life.

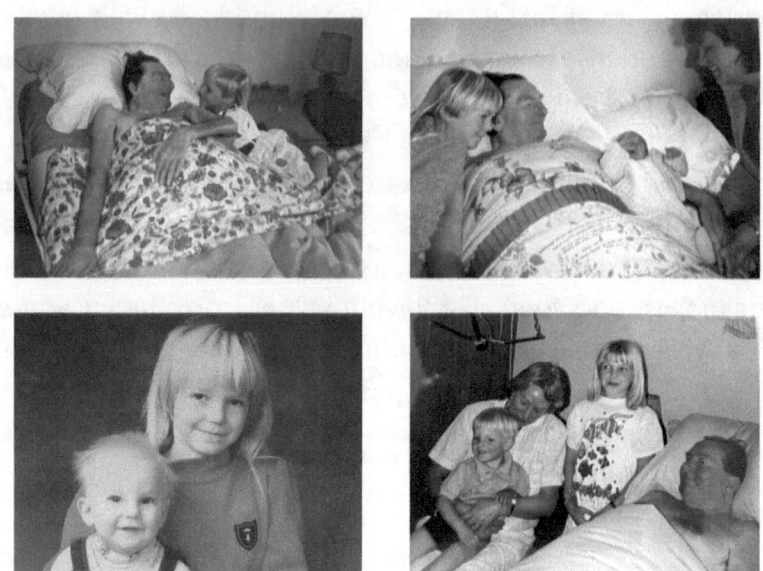

Danielle chatting with her Grandpa (top left)

Dad meeting Luke for the first time (top right)

Proud Grandparents (bottom right)

Danielle, aged 6 yrs, and Luke, aged 10 months (bottom left)

a. Luke proudly holding the first fish he caught 'all by himself'

b. Danielle's Year 12 graduation ball with Mum and me

Autumn

Autumn's Wisdom

In hues of amber and golden grace,
Autumn arrives with a gentle embrace.
Whispering winds, so crisp and cool,
A season of wisdom, a tranquil school.

Leaves that flutter, like the pages of time,
As nature prepares for its grandest prime.
Beneath the boughs, I stand in awe,
Witnessing life's metamorphosis, completely enthralled.

I've journeyed far and seasons have passed,
Matured like the oak, I am rooted steadfast.
And now I watch my children bloom,
Their wings unfurl, ready to consume.

With pride and joy, my heart overflows,
Seeing them flourish, as time quickly goes.
They tread their own paths, their dreams they all chase,
Becoming adults and finding their place.

The purpose that now fulfills my soul,
Of nurturing their spirits and making them whole.
I have guided them through life's winding road,
Shared wisdom learned; a love bestowed.

And as I dream, envisioning their tomorrows,
I send them my wishes, to be free from sorrows.
May they all find love, both gentle and true,
And cherish the moments, in all that they do.

Seasons of My Life

For one day will come when I'll hold their children dear,
And whisper those same lullabies, chasing away fear.
A grandmother's love is unbounded and pure,
Embracing generations, a legacy to endure.

In the autumn of life, my heart remains bold,
As love multiplies, and never grows old.
Each grandchild is cherished, a precious treasure,
Embraced with love, so far beyond measure.

Now in this season, my heart does confide,
A tapestry woven, with love as my guide.
For Autumn's wisdom has shown me the way,
To love wholeheartedly each and every day.

- Anne James

CHAPTER 7

Divorce, Love and Becoming a Step-Mum

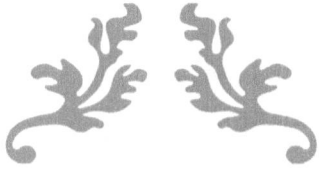

The next few years after my fortieth birthday, I lived through many changes and challenges. I struggled with my self-esteem and personal values and had to draw very heavily on the support of my 'village.'

There had grown a coldness and distance in my marriage. No longer were we working as a team, the closeness, care, and support had gone. I struggled with self-care; I became withdrawn and began to doubt my self-worth. An injury to my lower back halted my ability to work and be active for a time. There was judgement about my injury from many others and I was left to work it all out by myself. My mother was my strength during this time, she listened, showed compassion and her unconditional love. Others in my 'village' did not really know what was going on because I felt ashamed and became very private in what was really happening, including keeping what was going on from my own children, who were only eighteen and twelve at the time, mostly to protect them.

My marriage was faltering, something I never thought would happen to me. There were mistakes on both sides, we stopped communicating and I no longer felt I had the support of my husband. The work injury had placed a heavy burden on me, and I lost sight of being able to self-care. So, I stopped looking after myself, I comfort ate, gained weight, hid things, became afraid of conflict. To the outside world I put on a brave face but internally I was falling apart, and I did not really acknowledge that I was suffering from depression at that time.

Then the moment came when I realised that my husband no longer loved me and had found someone else. I was devastated, I fell apart. Somehow, I found the strength to support my children as we made the decision to separate. They were still young, finding their way and needed to have the support of both their parents. He was a loving and devoted father and still is, so through some heartfelt discussions we agreed to end the marriage. I remember packing up his belongings, becoming incredibly angry and considered destroying his things. I stopped, realising what I was about to do and how wrong it was and how this act would affect our children. That was something I did not want, it was not their fault, they were already struggling with the separation and the trust of their father. So, no matter what, I was not going to damage their relationship with their dad. That would be utterly unfair.

And for the first time in my adult life, I was living alone, as a single parent. My daughter was already living independently and studying

Divorce, Love and Becoming a Step-Mum

at university, and my son, was only a teenager and needing all our love, care, nurturing and guidance. I reminded them that what had happened with our marriage was not their fault and we both loved them. They still needed our combined love, guidance and support.

Did I find support for myself, no not at first, I put my feelings and emotions to one side and just made it through one day at a time. I eventually sought out some professional help and reached out to my 'village', I opened up about how I was struggling and with their care, compassion and love, slowly found my way back to myself.

The family home was sold, and there were no disputes about how things would be split, an amicable agreement between us about all things involved in a separation was decided. I then searched for a home of my own, that I could make my own and provide a home for my son as he began to spend his time equally between myself and his father.

2004 we divorced. No lawyers for custody battles, everything 50/50 and one night at work and on a break, I applied for our divorce, or as I commented to my work colleagues when asked what I was doing; "I am doing my divorce.com.au." Funnily, the day our divorce became final was, of all dates, the 4th of July (Independence Day).

Did I struggle financially? yes, and I made some poor choices and got into debt. I did take that step of eventually seeking help and slowly sorted everything out, this took several years but still I kept this to myself and, until writing this down, I do not believe most of my 'village' was fully aware.

Then, in 2005, a few days after returning from a trip to New Zealand, I woke one morning to neck, shoulder pain, and an inability to move my right arm. The pain was like a red-hot poker going from my neck and down to my right shoulder. I suspected what was happening. A call to my GP and his urgent call to a Neurosurgeon saw me driving one armed for an MRI and an immediate review with the neurosurgeon. No work from that day and a date was set for urgent surgery. You see, I had two prolapsed discs in my cervical spine that were pressing down on my spinal cord. I was scared as I knew what this potentially meant for me.

Home comes my daughter, dropping everything and with my mother and son, caring and supporting me, she and Mum became my taxi drivers, my cooks and my confidantes. I drew on my strength and sense of purpose to get through. There was one moment only when my fear overcame me. It was the morning of my admission to hospital; I was in the bathroom getting ready when I suddenly broke down; I dropped to the floor and sobbed and sobbed and sobbed. Then that wonderful inner voice said, "Enough of this, get up, pull yourself together and just get on with it." And that is what I did. Long surgery, cages and plate in, neck brace on, and a slow but steady recovery back to full health. Life moved on, I was now independent and had a sense of freedom.

I had drawn on my strength of purpose to forgive myself, love myself again, to be honest with myself, to find my own truth, and to be kind to myself. I was managing my weight, exercising, had found hobbies I loved, and with this new (or should I say rediscovered self) I had a renewed sense of purpose and joy in life.

Then a phone call in early October 2005 came out of the blue from one of my close friends, Iain, whom I had known since we were teenagers and was part of my 'village.' He was working and living overseas at the time, divorced, sending home money to support his children and coming home at regular intervals to see them. His ex-wife was critically ill, her family was not communicating with

Divorce, Love and Becoming a Step-Mum

him and had split up his children between various family members. He was at a loss, stuck and did not know what to do. There were long phone conversations at all hours to listen to him and support him over the few days until he could get home. A pledge to him to visit her in hospital with another of our friends occurred. She was dying and her family were very angry and blaming him.

A side note here; I have spoken with Iain and his children about putting all of this down as it was a devastating time, and the children were very young. They have all said, "Go ahead as it is part of your story as well."

On my visit to her, it was obvious that she did not have long and during one of her more lucid moments, she charged myself and my friend to 'care for her children!' Little did I know at the time what that truly meant for me.

During and after the funeral we, as a 'village' rallied around Iain and his children. Iain had moved back home to care for his children, the international company he worked for had arranged for him to work from home which was a huge relief for him. We stayed in close communication, Iain often ringing me to discuss how he was doing and seeking advice regarding how to help his kids cope with the loss of their mother. Over the next few months, he and I grew closer, love developed, and I came to love his children, and then he proposed. We asked the children for their permission, and if they would accept me as their step-mother, the answer was a resounding 'yes.'

We set our wedding date for the 12th of March 2006. It was a wonderful, hot, sunny Autumn day, the setting chosen was the Conservatorium at the Hobart Botanical Gardens. The choice of our attendants was an easy one, our children, and for me, my son Luke to 'walk me down the aisle.' We were surrounded by those who mattered, who we loved and who loved and cared for us in return, our family and closest friends.

We discussed where we should live, his place or mine, or find a new home to share. No hesitation on my part, these children had been through enough, they were only eleven, nine, and five at the time. I would not remove them from the only home they had known and where their memories of their mother were, so, I moved in with them. I too had memories of their mother, she had been a friend to me and had been part of my 'village' too. I had known these children for all of their lives, was part of their 'village' and was Godmother to their son.

They are the children of my Autumn.

I knew there were going to be challenges in raising them, helping them deal with their loss and how to help them through this; to find themselves again and learn not to be afraid anymore, to learn to be children again, so I sort professional advice. I knew there was going to be trauma, grief, anger, struggles with understanding, conflict with new circumstances, and all of this has been experienced.

They needed to become children again, to be loved, nurtured, and guided. They also needed to have boundaries set, values to be nurtured and guidance on slowly becoming more independent over time and as they matured. This did bring about conflict, arguments even screaming matches and lots of slamming doors, hurtful words said and a lot of stress for me. I drew on my strength of purpose, compassion, love for these children, and boundless patience. I also needed to set my own boundaries about what was acceptable behaviour, and this too brought resentment and resistance from these children at first. Many times, my darling husband, Iain, said to me, "I don't know how you can stay; we are so much trouble and do not deserve you." Oh how wrong he was. It was not about whether or not they deserved me, I loved them all unconditionally and leaving did not ever cross my mind.

Keeping the memory of their mother alive was important to me, they would call her by her first name in front of me and I would gently remind them that she was and always would be their mum, I would never take this away from them. At first, I was called 'Annie' by them but slowly they each asked if they could also call me 'Mum.' How that melted my heart as I already saw myself as their other mother but would not push them.

And so, to each of them,

The Children of My Autumn

Bonnie, the oldest, she had become a 'mother' to her siblings during her mother's long illness, getting them up for school in the mornings, finding food for them, caring for her mother when she was unable to care for herself, and so there was a struggle to get her to let go of the mothering role and take on a sibling role and be a child again herself. We often clashed and it required a huge amount of patience, unconditional love and support to nurture and guide her. As she approached her teenage years, there were fights, temper outbursts, risk-taking behaviours and disrespect of herself and us. I knew she was struggling with her mental health and tried to get her professional help, but she refused to engage. The risk-taking behaviours and disrespect grew worse and culminated in one evening when I discovered she had self-harmed quite badly, slashing her forearms from wrist to elbow and then covering these up with bandages. She lost it, screaming, fighting us off and totally irrational. This was to the point where both ambulance and police had to be called and we had to hold her down to stop her from harming herself any further. The rest of this story is hers' to tell.

Through many years of mental health issues, finally, a diagnosis of Borderline Personality Disorder was made, and over the years she has managed to come to terms with this. She continues to struggle at times, though with love, compassion and boundless patience, my hope for Bonnie is that she eventually finds peace within herself. Today, Bonnie is a strong, independent, fiercely protective, and loving daughter and I am blessed with being able to call her my daughter.

Lachlan (Lockie) was just nine years old when his mother died, and he became a very lost boy. He would not talk about his mother and became very defensive and unaccepting when anyone else tried to discuss with him the circumstances around her death. Highly intelligent, introverted, a deep thinker, quick to anger and struggled with expressing his emotions, he would not accept professional help with working through his grief. All he would say was, "There is nothing wrong with me it is all of you." We tried desperately to reassure him that we did not think that there was anything wrong but that we were concerned for him and loved him very much.

Slowly, over time, he came out of his shell, and found some enjoyment in life again. He took up hobbies and started making life choices as he decided what he wanted to do. Music has always been his go-to place much like his father. He took up drums and, allow me an indulgence here, he is a 'wicked' drummer. Joining various bands, exploring heavy metal, Aussie pub rock and for a period until he left home he and his father (who is a pretty good guitar player) would jam at home, experimenting with blues and jazz sounds. This was where they truly connected.

Divorce, Love and Becoming a Step-Mum

Our home became a half-way house for his various band members, and I would always make sure they had a feed when with us. His closest friends seemed to be able to 'sniff out' my Sunday roasts, so I always made sure I had plenty of vegetables to go around. And it was with these young men that the phrase 'Mumma Bear' was also coined in reference to me.

As an adult, Lockie has been through loss and challenges of his own but has come through this with his own strength of character, purpose, and is making his way back to his true self. He is a mechanic; an awesome father and I am so proud of all that he has done and all that he is.

Neve was a tender five years old when her mother passed away. At this age her understanding of what had happened was just what you would expect. She did not really understand why her mum had gone away. So, one night I took her outside to look at the night sky just as I had done with my own daughter when her grandpa had died. I found Venus in the sky and said, "If you can't find Mum just look up, she will always be there looking over you and loving you."

She was the one that would crawl up onto my knee wanting comfort and love, and I gave this unconditionally to all three of them. I taught her what 'butterfly' kisses were. She had many nightmares, so to comfort her I would get her to close her eyes and imagine the unicorns were there chasing the monsters away—she loved unicorns. Neve too was unable to express her grief, and this would often come out in temper tantrums with screaming, uncontrollable crying, and total panic, and we would not be able to reason with her. Sometimes I just had to grab hold of her and keep her close until she settled. Sometimes she would not accept this and would disappear into her room which was always her safe haven. She would either curl up in a ball under the doona or hide in her cupboard but eventually she settled, would come out for hugs and slowly I was able to get her to talk about what was the matter.

During her teenage years, Neve continued to struggle with her anger and was quick to catastrophize things. It became easier to help her understand when she had calmed down, but slowly she began to pull away, and not just from me but her father as well. No hugs or kisses, no communicating or opening up about how she was doing or what she was doing at school and with friends. This was 'none of our business.' What to do? As difficult as it was, we had to let her go through this stage. It broke my heart watching her struggle with finding herself, to watch this sensitive, compassionate girl and how she could not love herself or be compassionate with herself and was always judging herself. Again, she would not engage with professional help as she refused to open up.

It was through her love of horses that Neve learned to trust again and began to find herself. At the age of eleven she approached a neighbour of ours and asked through a letter she dropped into their letterbox if this neighbour could teach her how to ride. And teach her she did, not just about horses but how to give and receive love unconditionally.

This naturally led to Neve wanting to join Pony Club and compete in eventing competitions. Iain and I became part of the horsey community and went on a steep learning curve. It was also the one place where, for a time, we were truly able to communicate with Neve. Neve has never lost her love of her horses and has two; Sam who is now retired from competing, and Cyril who she now competes with, that is, when he stops injuring himself!

We now watch on as Neve continues the journey to finding herself, owning her own truth, and believing in herself and it is

Divorce, Love and Becoming a Step-Mum

just a wondrous thing to see. Again, she is our close, loving, caring, compassionate daughter. She has purpose in her life, and she has become strong and independent. I have very frequent video calls from her discussing her days, and how she is doing, she asks for advice and seeks guidance, but it is only offered when she asks for it.

As I have gone from forty to now, my family has grown, they are all so wonderfully inclusive, and my own two children took these children of my Autumn into their family and hearts, and they all get on so well together; it warms my heart and I know they will all be ok.

We have all gone through change and challenge; there has been conflict, compromise, learning to bond as a family, and growth. Supporting each other, loving and caring, and we have become a crazy, wild, loud, loving and wonderful family. Yep, all quite normal and ordinary, and so amazing and unique in my eyes.

CHAPTER 8

Memories of Mum

Elizabeth Marie Trevarthen (nee Langman)
B 1933 – D 2006

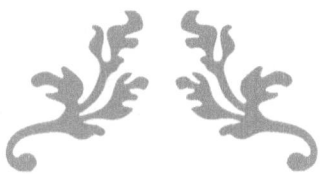

Mum was the strength of our family and the glue that held us all together.

She was a caring, sharing, strong and independent woman. She was serious when needed but had a wicked sense of humour, and right about now would be telling me to stop all the fussing and get on with it.

When I first started thinking about how I would write this chapter I suddenly realised I had already written it. I had penned the eulogy

Seasons of My Life

for Mum's funeral and had chosen to do it as a narrative, so I will now put down what I wrote then:

Much of what I recount here is in Mum's own words so it will be her speaking to you directly, and how special and precious that is...

How do you summarise a person's life? Woman, lover, wife, mother, grandmother, author, teacher of life, friend.

So, here goes... Hold on, sit down and get ready for one hell of a story...

Elizabeth Marie Trevarthen (nee)
Langman was born on the 24th of July 1933.

> 'It was a cold winter, that July of 1933 when I was born at the local hospital in Queenstown on the West Coast of Tasmania. My mother told me that I deprived her of her favourite breakfast, porridge. I wonder if that is the reason I grew up with a distinct dislike of porridge, as you will learn as I relate my life to you.'

Mum's parents moved to Sydney late in 1934 probably in the search of employment in the post-depression years, and they took up residence at 'The Avenue' sharing this hub of family with aunts and grandparents.

> 'The early years of my life are very dim to my memory, but I do remember my maternal grandfather and his care, taking myself and my cousin to and from Kindergarten on Anzac Parade. There are memories, too, of sitting at the balcony, perched on Grandpa's lap to watch the birds flitting from tree to tree. My grandmother was ever present; she was the hub of the family keeping the domestic scene viable while my parents, aunts and uncles went about their various jobs.'

Memories of Mum

The family moved to Wollongong late 1936 to the beginning of 1937 and it was there that Mum started school aged four, which was younger than normal at that time.

> 'My father worked for the local taxi company, and also joined the Citizens Army, I would help him clean his taxi but probably poured more water over myself than on the vehicle. It was fun to help him polish all the brass bits and pieces needed for his army uniforms. I soon learnt the meaning of 'elbow grease' when it came to shining his boots. To my child's eyes, he looked very handsome in his uniform, and I wonder now whether this was the catalyst for my association with people in uniform.'

With the declaration of war on the 3rd of September 1939, Mum's father was relegated to full-time duty and the family moved back to 'The Avenue'. Mum was enrolled at Crown Street Primary School but missed much of the first year due to illness.

> 'I succumbed to diphtheria on, of all days, my birthday. All was going well until the food arrived, when I complained of feeling ill. I remember lying on a couch in the lounge area, watching everyone else enjoying themselves with my mother and grandmother hovering over me in some anxiety. Next morning, I was whisked away by ambulance to Prince Henry's hospital and immediately placed in quarantine.'

The end of the year saw a return to health and a return to school. Air raid drills became the norm both at home and school, and porridge was the staple for breakfast...

> 'And I rebelled, sent off to school, not hungry but minus the porridge, only to return over the lunch break to be presented

> *with a bowl of cold porridge. Again, I would refuse, then back to school. First course of the evening meal for me was... you guessed it...that same cold bowl of stodgy porridge.'*

During this time my grandma decided to have Mum taught the piano and she took to it with such confidence that by the age of twelve she was ready to take the A. level music examination which would have qualified her as a music teacher.

> *'Sixteen was the minimum, and here I was at twelve, thwarted in my desires. So, the bubble burst and my enthusiasm began to wane, but not my love of music."*

Meanwhile, the war raged on, and Mum and Grandma received infrequent communication from her father who was serving overseas and had not seen him at all since the start of the war. Then in March 1943, the family was reunited and although Mum's father was then posted to Queensland, the family were together more frequently, and Mum continued her education at Sydney Girls' High School. With the end of the war, the family holidayed in Tasmania to visit with Mum's father's family, and on their return to NSW, they moved back to Wollongong. When Mum's grandfather, Langman, died, the family moved permanently to Tasmania and settled in Dynnyrne.

> *'On good advice from one of my aunts, I was enrolled at the Remington Business College. And after graduating I took up my first position in the big world of business. This was in the offices of Brownell's, now Myers, and how glamorous I thought it was to be working for a prestigious department store. But, oh! how boring it was typing envelope after envelope, day after day! I would give Mum my pay packet, untouched, which was three pounds per week, and she in*

Memories of Mum

> *turn, would hand me my bus fares and lunch money to tide me over for the week. Little did I know that the remainder was banked, a little nest-egg for later, such was the kindness of my mother's heart.'*

With the advent of the women's army being reformed in 1951, Mum joined, with her parents blessing, the Women's Royal Australian Army Corps and so began recruit training at Point Lonsdale on Port Phillip Bay, Victoria.

> *'Recruit training was a shock to the system. Reveille at 5:30 AM lights out at 10:30 PM and in between times 'make and mend' or 'hot maintenance,' for the uninitiated of army jargon, route marches, lectures, more route marches, and more lectures. Oh! Our poor, blistered feet!'*

Mum's first posting was to Brighton Army Camp, Tasmania, where her office skills were soon put to good use by becoming a payroll clerk and it was there that she met her first true love.

> *'Michael was tall, dark-haired, and very handsome. And we had many wonderful days together. On some Saturday nights we would walk four miles to the Coronation Hall in Bridgewater to dance the night away and then walk those four miles back to camp. On other weekends we would travel through to Launceston, Michael on his motorbike, and I with mutual friends. Then, tragedy struck at Easter of that year. After dropping me off to connect with a tram into Hobart, Michael met with a fatal accident just thirty miles from his parents' home. I was devastated. I remember curling up in my mother's lap to cry my heart out. But my life continued; to keep busy, was the answer and there was no shortage of duties to be done. Some may*

say I was on the rebound, but I do not. I then met my life's love, Anthony Rex Trevarthen. It was not the most romantic of meetings, for he was a patient at the camp hospital, and a national serviceman at that! Relationships between staff and trainees was strictly taboo, but our romance did not begin at that time. I was recovering from a serious operation at St. John's Hospital when six lads from camp paid me a visit. One of them was Tony and something electric seemed to spark between us.'

By that time, Dad had joined the permanent army and was an instructor, so their romance was not frowned upon…

'My roommates, ever curious, took an interest in my courtship. They even counted the times we went out before Tony kissed me goodnight, it was six times. The cheers that went up when I revealed all was tremendous.'

Dad graduated on the 25th of June 1953 and Mum accompanied his parents to the graduation parade…

'I was bursting with pride as I watched Tony command that parade. This was his honour as dux of that graduating class and also later at the prize presentation when he was awarded the Governor General's medal. That evening, at the reception, before the graduation ball, Tony slipped a solitaire diamond ring on the 4th finger of my left hand. The pledge of troth for the rest of our lives. And at midnight, I pinned the pips on the epaulettes of Tony's uniform, thus making him an officer and a gentleman, as he was in every sense of the word. Though not married, it seemed to me we were bonded together from that moment.'

Memories of Mum

Mum and Dad set the date of their marriage for the 11th of December 1954. It was a full military wedding with all the men in dress uniform and even six of Dad's fellow officers taking it upon themselves to give the happy couple the traditional sword of honour arch as they left the church. And so began their married life, and for Mum, the life of an army officer's wife.

> *'Knowing that the posting was in the offing, we were not surprised when that announcement was made. However, the excitement deepened when told we were off overseas, to exotic sounding Malaya for two years! But first, there were preparatory months ahead for Tony, intensive training and becoming acquainted with his troops. Thus began our nomadic life in the army.'*

Mum and Dad also made many firm friends during this time, and it was with one of them that Mum shared a very frightening moment during their passage to Malaya on board the SS New Australia...

> *'One balmy evening my friend and I were leaning on the ships rail, singing 'Tammy' when we saw ship lights coming towards us, zigzagging. Then a loud crash! The ship, a French tanker, had collided with us and put a great hole in the side of our vessel, no loss of life, but it was pretty scary at the time. The freshwater tanks had been damaged and we had lost an anchor. We spent three days off Thursday Island, swinging on one anchor, each morning we had no idea which way the ship was pointing. The Navy and Army engineers managed to repair the hole sufficiently for us to continue on to Singapore, but nothing could be done for the freshwater tanks. We drank tea and coffee made with salt water, and showered in saltwater using special soap, not the nicest of feelings. The engineers rigged up means*

of de-salination of the seawater for pregnant mums and children. The rest of us survived on cordial, and for the fellas...lots of beer!'

1959 saw Mum and Dad return to Australia, Dad going to Brisbane and Mum to Tasmania to visit with her parents, but she soon joined Dad for one of the few Christmases they would spend on their own. They had begun to doubt that they would ever become parents, so were thrilled when Mum discovered she was pregnant. With Dad's many commitments to the army, the decision was made for Mum to return to Tasmania for the birth of their first child, as she would have the support of her parents there.

'At 3:00 AM on the morning of the 9th of November 1960, Dad was apologising for all the potholes he had to negotiate on our way to Calvary Hospital. My response, "I don't care about the potholes, just get me there, and quickly!"' (This is what she wrote but I bet the language was slightly more colourful than that!)

Dad was not to see his first born, me, until a month after my birth and after Christmas spent with Dad's parents in Burnie, the new family moved into married quarters in Mornington.

'Whilst in Mornington, Tony tried to teach me to drive. This turned into a disastrous exercise, for it began to create arguments between us, with Tony giving up in disgust! Not to be outdone, I was determined to learn and sought the services of a driving school. Six weeks later, I was the proud holder of my first licence. But the first time I took our car out on my own, I was too scared to go too far, just 200 yards around the corner to a friend's house and back again. Tony roared with laughter when I told him where I had been!'

Memories of Mum

The next posting saw them once more returning to Sydney and to the haven of 'The Avenue' until the house became available in Kingsgrove and there they lived until a new posting, this time to Port Moresby, New Guinea the year now 1965. Dad went on ahead with Mum and me following three months later. Towards the end of 1965, Mum again discovered that she was pregnant.

> 'Our new baby was tardy in deciding to put in an appearance, so my doctor decided to hospitalise me for inducement, both surgical and medical. But with no result. After three days, Wendy decided to do it all by herself, and was born at 4:40 PM on Saturday the 9th of July 1966.'

Whilst in New Guinea, Mum took up employment with the PNG Electricity Commission and they employed a local lad by the name of Philip.

> 'He was only a young boy of nineteen and became Wendy's hero. Sometimes I felt Philip would rather play with Wendy than do his chores, but he managed to keep everything up to scratch.'

Mum and Dad took advantage of the opportunity of staying in New Guinea to holiday at many places around the island and one such journey was to Wau in the central Highlands involving a car, plane ride and bus trip to get there.

> 'The flight took us from Jacksons Airport along the coastline in a westerly direction, then to turn due north, flying through a channel between high, precipitous mountains to the strip at Bulolo. It seemed as though the wing tips would touch those mountains on either side. Apart from the pilot, we were the only other Europeans on board, our six other companions

> were indigenous with small livestock, chickens and pigs, that added to the interest. Then a hair-raising minibus ride from Bulolo to Wau over a very narrow dirt road, with a steep drop into a ravine on one side, and tall mountains on the other. Oh! The children loved it, but I was scared stiff.'

1969 saw another posting, back to Australia and staff College in Queenscliff, Victoria. So, Mum was charged once more with packing up and safely moving her family. At the end of this time Dad was posted to 3bn RAR, Woodside, South Australia and it was from here that he saw service in Vietnam, so he and Mum were separated once again. But before Dad left for his tour of duty overseas, they shared some wonderful family times together.

> 'Sunday nights became fun nights for us. After a traditional roast meal in the middle of the day, something light and easy was the order for our evening meal. The girls and Tony converged in the kitchen while I made fresh pancakes to my grandmothers' recipe. As fast as these came out of the fry pan, they were snatched away, slathered with butter and devoured! All of this amidst lots of laughter and chatter.'

October 1971 saw Dad back with Mum and his girls, but first a second honeymoon of just twenty-four hours was in order...

> 'I waited and waited for Tony to alight from the aircraft, what I did not realise was, since he was first to board, he would be the last to disembark! But, at last, there he was, and I raced into his arms. Oh, how wonderful it was to have him close again.'

And so, our family was reunited once more, but had hardly settled into a normal routine when Mum was again to pack up and get ready for another move, this time back to Tasmania for what was to be their final posting. Then, in 1973, Dad announced that he was retiring from the army, and for the first time we went house hunting for our very own home.

> 'And so, we found 17 Pascoe Ave, Claremont, with Anne and Wendy falling in love with the house at first sight, and Wendy immediately claiming the attic rooms as her own. The move to our first home was made in January 1974. It was most wonderful to have space to spread our belongings and ourselves in this place which had so much atmosphere. I knew that we would be so happy here, our very own haven.'

It was now that Mum and Dad joined the local RSL and Mum took up long-term employment with Lysaght Pty Ltd as secretary to the state manager.

> 'There was great excitement in 1976 when I won a considerable amount of money in Tatts Lotto. What was I to do with this windfall? A family conference solved that question, we would go cruising, and cruising we went...twice.'

1977 through to 1983 saw many changes in Mum and Dad's lives. Wendy and I were growing up, I had started my nursing training, then got married, and Wendy was well established in school and an avid sports person.

> 'The months passed by into Wendy's final year of high school and her 16th birthday. For this I managed to arrange a surprise party for her. Oh! The surreptitiousness of it all, but the look of utter surprise on her face was well worth the effort, and her friends went along with all that I asked of them.'

Seasons of My Life

Another wonderful event was the birth of Mum and Dad's first grandchild and what proud grandparents they were.

> 'The great day arrived. I felt honoured yet humbled to be allowed to witness Anne's labour... The moment of birth was a wondrous experience for me, as my beautiful granddaughter, Danielle, came into the world.'

And this is how she felt about all her grandchildren, cherishing every one of them and how proud of them she was…

This is where Mum left off her story mid 1983 for the events that took place over the ensuing months became another story and she charged both my sister and I with continuing that story.

And so, the years rolled by to the year 2006, it was both a wondrous and a sad year. Mum had seen both her girls settled and happy again, then the devastating news of Mum's illness in early November rocked all our worlds. But Mum, ever stoic, continued to care about her family. Throughout it all she never lost her sense of humour and shared many a joke with us and with the wonderful staff of the Gibson unit. In her final hours we all shared some precious moments with her, and one that we shared at her eulogy and is now placed on Mum and Dad's headstone was when Wendy's daughter broke down and cried…Mum turned to her, held out her arms and said:

> "Do you know the song 'Don't Cry for Me Argentina'? Well, don't cry for me, smile for me. Cry for you, cry for peace in the world, but smile for me…"

And that was the measure of my Mum, always caring, always there for her family, to love, comfort, nurture and guide them, even in her final moments.

Reflections

As a single beam of light,
Is reflected from the sun,
She warms our hearts.
Age is not a vast barrier,
For she is simply, matured, aware,
She is the wisdom, our knowing elder,
Yet her heart is alive with youth.
Now her fingers live with the keys
That tell a sensitive history,
To reveal her clear vision of family.
Her life, her strength, her sun
Providing warmth and light each day,
Then guides her through the night,
As beams reflect from the moon.
Like the sun, she was home alone,
But not alone in her heart,
For his love lived within her,
And now their love will go on together
Forever more.

- Danielle Newman (her granddaughter)

CHAPTER 9

Becoming a Grandmother

I am Nannie Anne to all my grandchildren and feel so privileged and proud to be called this.

Finding out I was to become a grandmother for the first time was truly magical. I was excited, felt so honoured and could not wait to start this next chapter in my life. Then to become a grandmother not once but *six* times now is astounding. Each time I have fallen instantly and unconditionally in love with these beautiful children of my children.

Becoming a grandmother has taught me so much and I learn new things about myself each time I am with them. To slow down and be in the moment, to take each day as it comes. To enjoy and embrace the simple pleasures, to have endless time and patience. I have allowed the child in me to come forward again as I get down on my knees to play with them (which is no simple task anymore), to be silly, to sing loudly, to dance, to have fun. Then there are the quiet moments; reading to them, listening to how their day/week has been when I visit, or they visit or during phone conversations. As a grandmother I don't just say 'that's nice' when my grandchildren show me something or tell me their exciting news. I jump up (or in my case, get up unsteadily!), throw my arms up, clap, laugh in excitement with them, say 'that's so good' or 'well done' and then they get a big bear hug, each and every one of them.

I would always sing to my children when they needed comfort or calming or to help them get off to sleep. A simple tune called 'Daisy, Daisy' where I would repeat the refrain over and over. I have also done this with each of my grandchildren and it brings such a sense of peace, warmth and real connection to see their little faces relax, look up into my eyes with such trust, and then when they finally sleep. That special, quiet moment between a grandmother and her grandchild is so precious.

Each of my grandchildren are unique individuals with their own special qualities that delight me.

My eldest grandson, Theodore Rex (Theo) born in 2010, a sensitive, loving, caring, and inquisitive young man, and during the writing of this book has just turned thirteen and is now in high school and doing so well. He is an academic and a deep thinker, just like his mother, and dare I say, just like me and my mother. He also has a love of sport, playing cricket and basketball. Ninja warriors has been one of the things he has loved and when visiting we were often asked eagerly to watch as he went over the courses that he and his dad would set up either in the hallway or out in the yard. He loves

Becoming a Grandmother

motor racing and hopes to one day be an engineer working in the F1 racing industry. Such wonderful purpose and I know he will get there no matter what he eventually does decide upon.

My beautiful granddaughter, Leila Joan born in 2014, Danielle's second child, was also a very inquisitive baby and toddler, a bit of a tomboy at times and not afraid to compete with her brother, she will turn nine this year. She also soon showed she had an artistic streak; dancing and performing for us all at the drop of a hat. She can be shy but as she has gotten older, she has blossomed and become more outgoing. She does rhythmic dancing, drama school, and is even learning the saxophone. I love going to her events or receiving pictures and videos. Leila does not yet know what she wants to do, and that's okay because there is still plenty of time. It's time now just to let her be a child and, with guidance, explore her own world. And exploring she is. As a family, we just recently witnessed Leila starting her own faith journey with the decision to be baptised. She was given the freedom to have control over her own life, just as Theo has, with discussion, guidance and support from their parents.

After these two I thought it would be quite a while before there were any more grandchildren, then out of the blue and within six weeks of each other, both Luke and Lockie announced they were unexpectedly going to become fathers. Yes, a surprise, but both babies very much wanted.

Lockie was first and there were discussions around his feelings of how good a father he would be at just twenty-two years old—he has always been the doubter—but he knew he very much wanted this baby. Then Luke, I had privately despaired if he would ever become a father as I knew he would make a wonderful dad. Lots of support and excited anticipation particularly as both wanted to know the gender of their babies – two little boys. Then tragedy struck...

Lockie and his partner had gone for their anatomy scan at sixteen weeks, and to find out the gender of their baby. Such an excited call to receive from him to let Iain and I know it was a boy! This followed by the news that all was not well. I accompanied them to the doctor's office for support. The diagnosis was Hydrops Fetalis, a rare, serious and life-threatening condition where there is a build-up of fluid in two or more body compartments of the foetus. For this little grandson, it was most severe, and he would likely not survive. How shocked and saddened we all were. How could I support my son and his partner, I thought. The only way was with love, support, compassion and honesty. That evening as we sat discussing the news and I began to re-explain all that had been said in layman's terms, there was the desperate question of what should we do? The only response I could give was to focus on their baby, take each day, one at a time, to have hope and to name their son. With no more than a moment's hesitation, this is what they did; he was named Hunter Iain Michael. There were decisions to be made and hard ones at that, however, nature made the decision for everyone, and our dear little grandson was born sleeping at twenty-three weeks' gestation.

Iain and I were overseas at this time and felt so hopeless not being able to be there for our son and his partner. His siblings were all amazing and our dear friend, Kim, was there also to support them all and to keep us informed of everything that was happening. We arrived forty-eight hours after this little man had passed away. My son, so grief stricken, so lost, not knowing what to do next. Iain and I set our emotions to one side to help support our son and his partner, organise the funeral and all other things. Our 'little boy blue'—always young—would have been four years old now and will forever be young in my heart.

Becoming a Grandmother

Don't think of him as gone away,
His journey is just begun.
Life holds so many facets,
This earth is only one.
Just think of him as resting,
From the sorrow and the tears,
In a place of warmth and comfort
Where there are no days and years.
Thinking how he must be wishing
That we could know today,
How nothing but our sorrows
Can really pass away.
And think of him as living
In the hearts of those he touched,
For nothing loved is ever lost
And he was loved so much.

- Unknown Author (This is the poem I read out at his funeral and was taken with permission from the 'Bears of Hope' website)

Seasons of My Life

Later that same year there was joy again within the family when Luke's little boy, Kohbi Maxwell, was born hale and hardy. He and our 'little boy blue' were going to grow up together, cousins and playmates, but that was not to be.

Seeing my eldest son holding his firstborn, feelings of love, joy and amazement came over me. Here was his hope and dream, nestled so close in his arms. An easy-going infant, loved by all. He has grown into an inquisitive, outgoing, polite and fun-loving little boy, the apple of his father's eye and so like his father in so many ways.

This was in November 2019, and we all know what struck the world some few weeks later, COVID-19, lockdowns, families separated and so it was with our family.

Weekly video calls became the norm but did not replace being able to see them and hold them and be with them all. I thought I would miss out on so much with my grandchildren, but my wonderful family made sure this did not happen. Always there were messages, short videos of each of my grandchildren, and a few wonderful notes from my granddaughter sent to me, telling me how much she loved and missed me. When things opened up here in Tasmania in mid 2020 the first thing we did was arrange a family get together, half-way between Hobart and Launceston at the park in Campbelltown. A crisp, clear cold day with plenty of hugs, air kisses, masks on except when outdoors. Bike rides for the children, playing on the swings, chasing the birds around, playing catch with the ball, all the things we had missed out on. How it warmed my heart to be able to do this.

Then joy, oh joy! 2021, and again, "Surprise, Mum! You are going to be a grandmother again." First from Lockie then from Luke.

Becoming a Grandmother

Our rainbow baby: for Lockie and his partner, anxious days and ever watchful during this pregnancy, but all was well and in the September another very precious grandson was born, Paxton Brody Reid. How the tears flowed when I saw Lockie so gently and proudly holding his son so close to his chest.

When Paxton was about six-months old, Lockie's relationship with his partner had become tenuous at best and suddenly he found himself a single father of an infant son. By this time, we had moved to 'Rosebank Cottage', and he would come up each weekend with Paxton for guidance and support as he learnt how to care for his son. I am so proud to say that through all his tragedy and grief, his doubts in himself, he is raising this beautiful boy with so much love and care. This little one, obviously torn between two very different households and values, all we can do is give all our love unconditionally. He is such a sweet boy, coming out of his shell slowly and loves being outside in my garden when he is here.

And finally in December of the same year my youngest grandson arrived, Nathaniel James. So, my eldest son, Luke, now had *two* boys of his own, and this one loves his cuddles and Nannie kisses, he is cheeky, also inquisitive, laughs a lot and natters away when concentrating on something.

These three grandsons are my three little boys and I love having them here, watching them play outdoors; Luke's two quite boisterous and outgoing and our rainbow baby, Paxton, happy to watch on and slowly explore this garden in his own time.

All our grandkids will grow up close cousins and the best of friends with their parents instilling their values, teaching their children about love, respect, kindness and caring and will support them in all their endeavours.

Seasons of My Life

I am so looking forward to watching all of my grandchildren grow and develop. I know each one will be lovingly supported by their parents in all that they do and all they want to be.

Suffice it to say that I am one very proud Grandmother.

I love you all 'To the moon and back!'

Iain and I exchanging vows, March 2006

Our children were our attendants. L to R back: Simon, Iain, Me, Luke and Danielle. L to R front: Bonnie, Neve, Lockie.

a. Danielle and Josh with Theo and Leila (top left)

b. Lockie and Paxton (top right)

c. Luke and Emily with Kohbi and Nathaniel (bottom left)

d. Neve and Bonnie (bottom right)

Iain and Me with our Grandchildren. Christmas 2021

Winter

Winter's Blessing

Now in the winter of my life, I stand tall and strong,
A journey through time, where reflections belong.
With grace, wisdom, and values I hold dear,
I embrace this season without any fear.

As snowflakes fall, my memories surround,
A tapestry of moments cherished and profound.
Each chapter written, in the book of my years,
Etched with laughter, and sometimes tears.

Gathered 'round the fire, my family and I,
Sharing stories and love, as time drifts by.
In these precious moments, we find our true selves,
Blessed with the bond that forever dwells.

Through thick and thin, we've weathered all storms,
Unified by love, our hearts will keep warm.
Happy or sad, we stand side by side,
In the winter of my life, united we stride.

The challenges we face, the successes we achieve,
Lessons learned, and dreams yet to be revealed.
I pass on my wisdom, the lessons I've learned,
To the ones I hold dear, as their path is discerned.

For the winter of my life is not yet at an end,
But a new beginning, as I transcend.
With a heart full of gratitude, I welcome the days,
To live with purpose, in a myriad of ways.

Seasons of My Life

So let the winter winds whisper their tune,
As I dance with time beneath the silvery moon.
I'll embrace each moment, with love as my guide,
In the winter of my life, I'll abide.

- Anne James

CHAPTER 10

A Life-Changing Moment

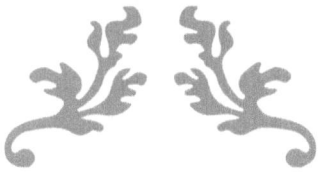

It was a cool, crisp, clear day, on the 8th of April 2018...Oops! It sounds like I am writing a fiction story here. But no, not fiction, all fact and the start of an illness and journey that brought great change, challenge and life decisions for myself and Iain.

I was at my desk at work ordering the influenza vaccines for that year's clinics in preparation for the upcoming flu season when I quite suddenly began to feel 'blah' (yes, an official medical word!). A wave of tiredness washed over me with body aches, joint aches, a pounding headache, and when I took it, a temperature reaching 40 degrees Celsius.

Knowing I needed urgent medical review, but struggling to rise from my chair, I contacted one of the reception staff. She got the other nurse on duty to assess me first who then called in one of the doctors. When the doctor came in and assessed me, I was ordered home. By this time, I felt so ill that they called Iain to come and get me. I was ordered straight to bed, and to come back in for a review the next day, or off to the hospital if I became any worse.

Stubborn me, I refused the hospital and Iain became my nurse that night. When I went back for review with my GP the next day, a provisional diagnosis was made of influenza with swabs taken for confirmation then sent home to bed again. By this time, I had no appetite and could barely move but still I refused hospital review. I felt worse twenty-four hours later so a barrage of urgent blood tests, or as I affectionately call them, serum everything, were ordered, and a review booked for the following day, only to be rung later that same day to say yes, I did indeed have Influenza B and my test results had come back as very abnormal. Blood cell counts were way off, along with many others, and my kidney function tests being the only ones that were normal… I can say with full honesty that I was scared but too ill to really register the results. I know my doctor was worried, and still remember the look of concern on Iain's face.

This began the daily tests to make sure blood levels were improving and improve slowly they did. Because they were so abnormal further investigations ensued with more blood tests and scans. There was an urgent review with a Haematologist at first, as a condition called Monoclonal Gammopathy of Uncertain Significance (MGUS) surfaced, this was investigated because of my white blood cell count and the discovery of something called paraproteins (immunoglobulin proteins that are produced by a clone of plasma cells in the bone marrow) being found to be elevated—a mouthful I know and a weird sounding diagnosis. Iain, ever the one to want as much information as possible, became distressed reading that

A Life-Changing Moment

this could lead to Multiple Myeloma, a type of blood cancer, I was very quick to reassure him that the chance of this was very low indeed, but I don't think he believed me until he was given the same reassurance from the Haematologist. I continue to have my paraprotein levels checked annually as a precautionary measure.

I also received a diagnosis of ITP (Idiopathic Thrombocytopenia Purpura) – there I go again with another mouthful. This one because of my platelet count dropping significantly, probably in response to the viral infection. (As health professionals, we would often joke that 'idiopathic' meant we were idiots, we don't know! It really means 'of no known cause').

I would get bruises at the drop of a hat and had to watch out for bleeding. This too improved over about three months and has never been a huge concern since but is still checked whenever I have blood tests.

I was well enough to return to work after two weeks but continued with lingering fatigue and brain fog and then I began to have worsening joint soreness and stiffness mostly in my hands, eventually waking one morning about six weeks later with swollen, painful joints and fingers to such an extent I could not hold a knife, brush my hair or even use the keyboard at work without significant pain. It was thought these symptoms were likely to be a reactionary arthritis to the influenza infection which should resolve. However, it did not get better, and instead got worse and worse. Yes, there were more tests to rule out more things, but my results eventually came back as being RA (Rheumatoid Arthritis) factor negative, but my other inflammatory markers were elevated.

From there I went to see a specialist...

Seasons of My Life

A referral to a Rheumatologist was made and off I went with a list of my symptomology to that stage. By this time, I was also getting weird rashes, regular fevers, and strange nodules on my fingers. I also continued to have flares of joint pain and swelling both in my hands and feet.

I think I cried a little when I was in with my rheumatologist (my GP was constantly telling me this would all pass, but I knew better). She made a provisional diagnosis of Inflammatory Arthritis or Seronegative Rheumatoid Arthritis and began me on medication immediately. Of course, I had done my own research and with my nursing background knew the risks and benefits of these. It began with a high dose of Prednisolone to get my inflammation under control, and weekly injections of Methotrexate which I still administer to myself to this day.

Then the infections started; at first it was hard lumps in my axilla (arm pit) which were very painful until they were drained. Horrible abscesses with cellulitis on my thighs and buttocks—with that came so much trouble being able to sit. These required medical interventions with incision, draining and antibiotics. You see, I was now immune-compromised by the RA given that it is an Autoimmune Disease, and the medication I had to take for it. Over time they have abated, but I keep a script on hand to start immediately if my temperature goes above 38 and I feel another bacterial infection has started. And during all this, Iain soon learnt how to drain and dress wounds as I could not reach a lot of them. Many a funny moment spent with me lying prone on the bed as he dealt with the wound. Lots of 'oh, yuck' and 'where has all this goo come from'...but do it, he did.

Next on the list of things that happened was, I began noticing changes to the sensation in my feet. At first on the soles which

A Life-Changing Moment

would feel numb but also sensitive to touch (a contradiction in terms, I know). A strange tingling sensation then appeared and by now I described the sensations as being like constantly walking on rough, wet sandpaper and that someone was pouring ice water on my feet. This began to then ascend to my mid-calves. I would also feel like I constantly had socks on, and at its worst, it felt there were tight bands around each of my toes, a big old G clamp tightening on my feet and that I was walking on broken bones.

Evenings were the worst for me as my feet would burn, and I could not stand to have the bed clothes on. To add insult to injury I also found I became quite stiff and stuck, unable to roll over without sitting up, or even needing to stand out of bed to change my position, all of which severely interrupted my sleep. My rheumatological symptoms were also not improving and I was having constant flares, which played havoc with my home life and work.

After further scratching of heads with my rheumatologist and myself, it was decided to trial me on Humira, but I did not tolerate this, so after careful discussion with my rheumatologist, I commenced another biological agent call Tocilizumab, or as Iain came to call it, "Anniefixumab." Indeed, for a period of about eighteen months I did improve but then it stopped working.

Now back to the nervy stuff, and off to the next specialist…

I was referred to a Neurologist in April 2019 and after discussion, history taking, physical examination and nerve conduction studies, a diagnosis was made of Small Fibre Polyneuropathy. Now, this one can be present in a few disorders, but for me, it relates to the damage done to my peripheral nerves due to the inflammation caused by the rheumatoid arthritis. Thank goodness, too, as I had been quietly scared 'shitless' that it was going to be another condition similar to what my dad had been diagnosed with all those many years ago. Unfortunately, there was no real treatment for the condition as the damage had already been done, and the only thing to do was to try and get the inflammatory processes under control with my rheumatologist. Management of symptoms was with nerve-pathway blocking medication at night to reduce the pain and burning sensations; however this help is limited. I continue to manage through medication and distraction and my disability from this added condition is something I have learnt to accept.

I was also noticing an increase in balance issues, muscle weakness and fatigue—no falls but I came close at times, so I started using a walking stick to help with my balance. When I also started noticing how fatigued my arms became with only driving short distances, and a couple of scary incidents of my feet slipping off the pedals and I not being able to get them back on quickly, I made the decision to stop driving. I did not feel I was a safe driver any longer and I would be devastated if I had an accident and hurt anyone. Iain became my permanent chauffeur. I did feel a sense of loss of independence as I could no longer jump in the car to go shopping by myself and no longer could drive to Launceston by myself to visit and do 'nannie duty' with my grandchildren. I am just so fortunate to have Iain, he was and continues to be, caring, patient, and will always take me anywhere I need to go and even, with much sighing, tag along behind me as I browse when shopping.

Then Vasculitis arrived, headaches, my temples became very tender to touch, blurred vision, eye pain, jaw pain when chewing and tinnitus. "Oh great!" both myself and my rheumatologist said. As the Tocilizumab was not appropriate for this added auto-immune condition, an application was made for me to start having IV Rituximab, a monoclonal agent that depletes B cells (a type of

A Life-Changing Moment

white blood cell) from the circulation. Simply put, adding another more targeted agent to help suppress my immune system to decrease the systemic inflammatory processes going on in my stubborn and uncooperative body. I am still on this medication along with my Methotrexate. My flares are less frequent, and infections are less prevalent. Nothing can be done about my small fibre polyneuropathy, and my vasculitis symptoms are more under control. One of the hardest things is that I have been left with a physical disability that does impede my daily life activities to a degree.

Through the journey from first having the flu to where I am now, it has not been easy, but throughout it all and with all the decisions made Iain has been there beside me, listening to me, supporting me, being my chauffeur, cook, cleaner, confidante. Naturally our relationship changed and there were many ups and downs, but we have stuck together and grown as a couple. I have been on a roller-coaster ride of emotions and change as well with learning how to balance work, life, and illness. Throughout this journey, I continued to work full-time as a nurse in general practice. My role was mostly as a patient educator, managing their journey with chronic disease and goal setting around the things they could do to help themselves. So, I applied this same goal-setting approach to management for myself to the best of my ability.

By the beginning of 2021 and after much urging from my doctors and others working with me, I realised that something had to give; firstly, I reduced my hours at work. Then the decision, with much discussion at home, was that I needed to stop working completely. This did not come lightly as I was the only income earner, Iain's position having been made redundant back in 2017. His redundancy package was generous, though, and saw us through with some tight budgeting. It gave him the opportunity to have the time to care for his own parents who were requiring more and more support, eventually leading to them moving to Aged Care, and he now had the time to take up all the things I struggled with or could no longer do at home.

Pain

Managing Pain is something I work on every day; simple measures such as stretching, massage, walking (although this is now limited for me due to the fatigue), gardening when able, simple medication and distraction. And I can no longer wear high heels or dance with my love. So, sensible shoes and we rock, holding each other to our music. I live with pain every day and have come to an acceptance and a way of living with it.

Fatigue and Brain Fog

These are my constant companions now. I recognise when I am affected, have learnt how to balance rest and exercise. Mentally, when I start to get brain fog, I giggle to myself at the silly stuff that comes out of my mouth, or my fingertips as I write, I call this 'hold on rented fingers' and I have trouble finding words at times, get them mixed up, or as I say, "I have my mords wixed up." Or I can't concentrate. This is the cue for downtime where I relax, read a book, or watch a bit of TV. Bed is early for me and a chance to let my body, mind, and soul recharge for the next day.

A recent funny incident occurred just the other day. When I am having downtime, I am also transcribing a work of fiction written by my mother several years ago. A marvellous dictate application as part of Word allows me to speak it. So serious and speaking part of the story where the main character is hung outside in a cage on the walls of the Tower of London. The scene described as being wet, windy, cold, she is bedraggled, and I should have said 'she sat shivering' but so seriously said 'she shat sivering.' Iain was in the room at the time and both he and I just about wet ourselves laughing at this!

Anger

Yes, I have been very angry at what has happened and the changes it has brought about. I have turned this around and used it as a positive energy to help me fight each day, to maintain my purpose in life and now take each day as it comes.

Changes in My Body and Appearance

When I look in the mirror, I see that I have changed physically, not just as the natural process of getting older, but I have become 'moon-faced' as a side-effect of my medication, which is worse when I need to use the prednisolone short-term to help with flares. There is weight gain as a combination of not being able to be as active as I would like and the medication. It is stable and not something I worry too much about now because I am still me on the inside.

Iain and I were only talking about this the other night, we discuss deeply at times and then we banter, feeding off one another's warped sense of humour. He said, "From a ragged, old, hag to being beautiful."

My reply, after blowing him a 'raspberry', was, "And I love you too. You old bugger." He has truly kept me sane through all of this.

Seasons of My Life

Depression

This often happens when someone is diagnosed with a chronic health condition, and I have not been immune to this. Not to the extent of needing counselling or medication but feeling very down at times and yes, a little sorry for myself. There were days when all I wanted to do was curl up under the covers and tell the world to just 'f.... k' off. The pain, stiffness, joint swelling, and brain fog would get so bad that I would sob my heart out. The only person who ever really saw this was Iain and I even shielded him from the worst of it all. Enough of that my inner voice would tell me and I focused on the things I could do, my relationship with Iain, and my family and drew on my values to help me get through.

And Now to Retirement

As I mentioned it was a hard decision for me as I loved my job and had not envisioned retiring for several years to come. There was also the concern of how to make it through to retirement age financially. We still had a mortgage and although there was money in our Superannuation, it would leave us with very little by the time we both reached pension retirement age.

It was mentioned to me several times that I should apply for the Disability Support Pension, and Iain for the Carer Pension, as he was doing so much for me by this stage. I hesitated, felt guilty and that I did not deserve to have this pension as I felt it was for people much worse off than me! After speaking with several professionals about this, I was urged to apply because it was appropriate, and I was eligible. I found the process very easy to work through and when it came time for my Social Worker phone appointment, I was asked to describe what I was like on my worst day and don't hold back, so I did not. At the end of the interview, I was told by the social worker, "Well you are certainly eligible, and I am going to tag Iain's application to yours for immediate assessment and approval." We were approved almost immediately, and it has taken so much pressure off us.

How am I now? At peace, happy, contented, doing the things that I love. A new passion for gardening. I am spending quality time with my family and staying connected with friends by the marvels of modern technology.

What does the future hold for me? I do not know but whatever it is I will embrace it. I have lived with my constant companion for a while now and I don't yet know what final path it will take. I do know it may shorten my life here on earth (maybe). Does this frighten me? yes, at first it did, but no longer. It is a part of my life and despite the ups and down, trials and tribulations has helped me to evolve, re-discover myself and my values.

CHAPTER 11

The Journey Continues...

I am now beginning the journey through the winter of my life, and I look forward to it wholeheartedly. It is a time of reflection, making memories with my family, enjoying time with them all and watching as each one of them learns, grows, and finds their own true selves.

The times when we are together as a family are so precious to me. Through thick and thin, happy and sad, challenges and successes, we are all there for each other, loving and supporting each other.

Iain and I have grown in our love and marriage. It has not been without challenges as we built this life together. Two different personalities, his so black and white and mine seeing all the grey areas in between. We are yin and yang to one another. His support through the last eighteen years is so appreciated. Both very passionate, our love has mellowed, and we are comfortable in one another's company, no need for long winded conversations about every and anything. The silences are just as meaningful. Often when we do discuss things, we have the same thoughts and ideas. Iain will comment, "It's a bit scary, just like you are reading my mind." We enjoy debating about different values, world events, and although our opinions may differ, we listen attentively and acknowledge each other's points of view. I always feel respected. We love discussing esoteric subjects, quite often this does our heads in, and, in particular when discussing Quantum Physics after watching a documentary, we will say to one another, "Is your head hurting yet!"

For many couples, it is vital they share the same bed at night, Iain and I certainly felt that way, however with how restless I became with all those symptoms I previously described, we both had very disturbed sleep and would wake up very grumpy and short-tempered in the morning. This was having an impact on our marriage, something we quickly realised, and after discussion decided to get a 'sleep divorce' and it was our best decision ever! It means Iain gets an undisturbed sleep and I don't have to try and lie still so as not to disturb him. I can get up and down as needed. There is still cuddle time, and as always, hugs and kisses, and coming together in the morning. And in fact, we both believe this has brought a new dimension to our relationship.

I have found that 'looking back to look forward' has new meaning for me now. It gives me clarity of thought; I have evolved as a person and am truly at peace with who I am and where my life will take me. By looking back, I have had time to pause, reflect, reassess and learn from all those lessons learnt over the years. My future is something I have yet to explore.

The Journey Continues...

Through the power of writing, I have embarked on a remarkable journey that has led me to a profound state of self-discovery. It is as if I have been granted a magical key, unlocking the doors to clarity of thought, an unwavering connection with my true self, and the depths of my creative spirit. In this process, I have become an author, not merely by putting pen to paper, but by experiencing a sudden moment of awareness that shifted the very essence of my mindset, almost unconsciously.

As my fingertips now move on the keyboard, weaving words and sentences into my story, I find myself transcending the boundaries of my existence. The act of writing has become an alchemical process, transforming the intangible musings of my mind into tangible expressions of my soul. Through the dance of language, my thoughts begin to take shape, taking flight from the recesses of my mind and finding their place on the page.

In this metamorphosis, I have discovered a profound belief in myself, a belief that permeates through every line, every paragraph, and every chapter. Doubt, once an unwelcome companion, has now been replaced by an unwavering confidence in my ability to create something meaningful, something that resonates with both myself and others who dare to embark on this literary adventure with me.

With each stroke of the keyboard, I traverse the landscapes of my inner world, unearthing hidden treasures and forgotten memories. My words have become the compass that guides me back to the core of my being, where my truest self resides. It is through this connection with myself that I have found solace, understanding, and a profound sense of fulfilment.

In this newfound identity, I embrace the boundless possibilities that writing offers. With each word I pen, I will step further into the realm of self-expression, realising that my voice does have the power to touch hearts, provoke thought, and spark change. I am an author, and with each stroke of my pen, I embark on a journey of endless exploration, both within and without.

I have travelled this path growing 'my garden of values' both within myself and seeing it planted, germinated, and flourishing in my own children and now grandchildren. I look forward to watching as they continue their journeys.

I love tending my own physical garden. I grow organically, with love and care, and yes, I talk to my plants and trees! I took on the task of learning how to grow organically and embrace the nature around me.

Waking up to beautiful sunrises, being present in the season's changes, listening and watching the bird life, insects and bugs. Getting excited when I see the pollinators descend. Looking on in wonder as I see the tips of bulbs breaking through the soil or the buds appearing on my flowers and fruit trees. The blossoms when they appear are magnificent and herald the fruit my trees will eventually bear that I can share with my family. Watching my vegetable seeds and seedlings come to life and grow. I get so excited at each change and when the flowers, fruit and vegetables start to really grow. Iain often catches me talking with my plants and trees as I go about my business in the garden, which he shakes his head at, and I laugh when I see the look on his face. We often joke about it using phrases such as, 'you have become the crazy garden lady' or 'do I need to call the 'little white van' to come and take you away.' To which I reply, 'I have been crazy all my life, not about to stop now.' He tells me this is part of why he fell in love with me.

I love nothing more than preserving, jamming, turning the tomatoes into all things wonderful, from eating fresh, on toast, grilled, baked,

The Journey Continues...

canned, made into passata. And at the end of the season, green tomato pickles just like my Nan used to make. I currently still have 5kg of tomatoes in the freezer ready to make more pickles and chutney at the end of this Winter.

Nothing gives me greater satisfaction than now seeing my pantry filling each year with wonderful home produce to have and to share, always with a reminder to my family; clean and bring back the jars and there will be more for you to enjoy.

We are settled now in our lovely home, Rosebank Cottage. Our garden is our love and legacy as is the 'garden' we have planted in our family. The values that were instilled within me by my parents and extended family, I now pass on to my future generations and my readers.

CHAPTER 12

Of Lessons Learnt and Lessons Taught

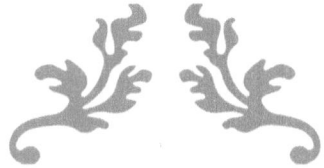

I have led a most wonderful and interesting life thus far and still have much to give, to learn about myself, to grow and evolve as a person. Having my own personal values and living my life according to those values has helped in all my relationships both personally as a wife, mother, sister, grandmother, friend and also in my professional life as a nurse.

Having these values helps you to influence your actions, your relationships and your lives. They help guide your decision-making and influence your personal development. They come from your childhood upbringing, your life experiences and culture. They can

Seasons of My Life

develop at any stage of your life and will evolve with time and lived experience.

Living your life with your values helps you to be true to yourself and gives you a sense of purpose in life.

Your values shape your personality, your goals in life and the actions and decisions you make as you live your life.

For me the most fundamental core values my parents taught me, I live my life with and have taught my children are:

Of Lessons Learnt and Lessons Taught

Love

*'You yourself, as much as anybody in the entire universe,
deserve your love and affection.'*
- Buddha

Love wholeheartedly, completely and unconditionally, it comes back to you 10-fold.

Learn to love yourself first for then you have love in abundance for all others. It is a choice and a way of relating to who you really are. To be able to not judge yourself poorly for your mistakes or losses, to move forward in life with love, confidence and happiness.

The love for and of my family is at my core and holds me up each day to move forward with joy and happiness. There will be struggles and challenges throughout life, however with love these can be overcome, and new lessons are learnt, sometimes without you even realising it.

My greatest love and joy is listening to my family of their lives and hopes.

Tell your loved ones that they are loved each time you see or speak with them.

When I see my grandchildren and hold them, they are enveloped in a huge bear hug and told 'I love you To the Moon and Back.' I often get the spontaneous response of 'I love you more' or even 'and a thousand, thousand times more.'

This fills my heart and soul with joy.

Seasons of My Life

What do I believe Love of self is:

- To accept yourself for who you are.
- That no-one is perfect; ditch that idea!
- You are unique.
- To be kind to yourself.
- To be grateful for all that you are and all that you have.
- To forgive yourself. We all make mistakes and have regrets. Learn from them and believe in your ability to grow from them.
- Allow yourself to be creative.
- Always remember who you are.

Of Lessons Learnt and Lessons Taught

Respect

*'Respect for ourselves guides our morals,
respect for others guides our manners.'
- Laurence Sterne*

*'Treat people the way you want to be treated. Talk to
people the way you want to be talked to. Respect is
earned, not given.'
- King Hussein Nishah*

I was taught to treat others as I would want to be treated and this is something that my parents showed in their daily lives. Never did I hear them put someone down or judge. They did talk about respectful differences of opinion, to be engaged and to listen actively.

They also taught me to respect myself first. I was taught by example and by conversation, always to treat myself with care, to stay true to my beliefs and values. I was encouraged to not compare or judge myself by comparing myself and my life with others and to accept myself for who I was.

I endeavoured to show and teach my children this same value by always encouraging them to act according to their beliefs and values, to surround themselves with like-minded people who would support and embrace them for just being who they were. To spend time and energy on what they were passionate about and to always do that which makes them happy.

My children were encouraged to have a routine, to stay connected with family and friends. It was important for them to have a hobby or passion, to stay healthy in mind and body. It was also important that they take time for relaxation, to unwind and recharge, to reflect.

Showing respect for others is something that was very important for me growing up and I encouraged my children to have this same respect by treating others as you would want to be treated. By being polite, patient, to show care and compassion. To actively listen and be engaged when in conversation. They were also encouraged to seek to understand others, to be curious and interested. To accept differences and respect other people's perspectives.

Compassion

'There are many interpretations of compassion, focussing on different aspects of our response to suffering. One way to categorize different types of compassion is by varying the focus of our response, including our feelings, actions, concern and intentions.'
- Paul Ekman

Be concerned for the person who is suffering. Help them through their suffering if you can do so. Listen empathically to them and be willing to engage with them on any level you are able, to help them through their suffering.

Why does compassion matter? By setting your emotions to one side you will be able to help in a practical way more actively. You are not trying to solve their problem or suffering but rather supporting them during their time of suffering. It does not have to be world changing but can be done through simple daily kindness.

I was taught this and then taught my children through example or getting them to put themselves in the other person's shoes.

Examples:

- Helping someone who has dropped their groceries or parcels to pick them up.
- Giving up your seat on public transport to someone who needs the seat, such as an older person, a pregnant woman, a parent carrying their baby, a person on crutches.
- Helping your family or friends to move house.

Seasons of My Life

- Watching a neighbour's house when they are away and watering their garden, collecting their mail.
- Preparing a meal for someone who is sick or injured.

Everyday things that we often do without thinking about it or letting our emotions get in the way.

Of Lessons Learnt and Lessons Taught

Honesty

'Honesty is more than not lying. It is truth telling, truth speaking, truth living, and truth loving.'
- James E. Faust

'No legacy is so rich as Honesty.'
- William Shakespeare

It is important to be honest with yourself and it is a hard thing to do. By being honest with yourself you can be honest with those around you. Reaching an understanding of yourself and exploring your own honesty can lead to a better understanding of 'why you are who you are.'

Being honest with yourself can be painful, you will feel vulnerable, and it can cause anxiety.

Take time each day to reflect not just on the past but also on the future. Don't leave anything behind that will cause regret in the future.

Being honest with yourself takes courage and self-awareness. It is challenging and will challenge you to take action and be courageous. It will lead to an improvement in your own health and happiness.

Be mindful and non-judgemental when you explore your feelings and reactions to the experiences you are living and seeing around you. Take notice of how you are thinking and feeling. Learn to truly listen to yourself to gain an understanding of your 'own truth.'

Living with honesty in your life leads to a sense of fulfilment and ability to be 'the best you, you can be.'

Integrity

*'Be Impeccable with Your Word. Speak with integrity.
Say only what you mean. Avoid using the word to speak
against yourself or to gossip about others. Use the power
of your word in the direction of truth and love.'*
- Don Miguel Ruiz

For me, this means having the quality of being honest and having strong moral and ethical principles.

Those that know you, know that you are dependable, loyal, honest, have good judgement, and respect.

There are many attributes of integrity; for me, the five that stand out the most are:

- Dependability: Showing that people can count on you, that when you commit to something you follow it through.
- Loyalty: Commit wholeheartedly and without reservation to those around you, 'your village.'
- Honesty: Always strive to be truthful. To be honest with yourself and others. This encourages you to have trust in yourself and that others can trust in you.
- Good Judgement: It is about learning to think things through and arriving at the best choice in decision-making situations. By showing integrity you will develop a keen sense of intuition and you will make good judgements more often.
- Respect: Learning to value yourself and other people, to accept others for who they are. By having respect, you build feelings of trust, safety, and wellbeing. Show respect for others, by being kind, courteous and to really listen to others.

Of Lessons Learnt and Lessons Taught

Some examples of everyday integrity would include:

- Refrain from sharing secrets and confidential information with others.
- Remain honest with yourself.
- Avoid gossiping about other people.
- Follow through on promises you make.
- Return found items without an expectation of receiving a reward.
- Admit when you are wrong.

Patience

'It is very strange that the years teaches patience - that the shorter our time, the greater our capacity for waiting.'
- Elizabeth Taylor

'It does not matter how slowly you go, as long as you do not stop.'
- Confucius

What for me is the meaning of patience? To be able to accept or tolerate delay, problems or suffering without becoming annoyed or anxious.

It takes a lifetime of learning to develop patience in oneself, and I believe that to gain patience we need to:

- Be mindful.
- Have self-control.
- Teach yourself to slow down and take your time with tasks.
- To put some fun in each day, choose an activity, have laughter in your life, enjoy life.
- Learn to actively listen to others, to hear their concerns, to be compassionate and tolerant.

When teaching children patience:

- Be mindful of their impatience and patient with them.
- Get them to name what it is that is making them impatient or frustrated.
- Listen to them, speak in a quiet calm voice, teach them to close their eyes and take a deep breath.

Of Lessons Learnt and Lessons Taught

- Teach them an understanding of the difference between excitement and impatience. An example of this is looking forward to their birthday or to Christmas. They are anxiously awaiting that day, they're looking forward to the presents that they will receive, the party, to their birthday cake. Get them to talk about how they're feeling, what things they would like to do on the day. Get them to count down the days to that event, this will slow them down and give them the enjoyment of looking forward to that event.

Tolerance

'In order to have faith in his own path, he does not need to prove that someone else's path is wrong.'
- Paul Coelho

'Resolve to be tender with the young, compassionate with the aged, sympathetic with the striving and tolerant of the weak and wrong. Sometime in life you will have been all of these.'
- George Washington Carver

I was taught to accept beliefs or behaviours that are different from my own even though I might not agree with or approve of them.

Teaching my children about tolerance over the years has also taught me to be much more tolerant and accepting of others' beliefs and opinions even if they do not align with my own.

I have also learnt that it is sometimes better to hold your tongue and walk away.

Ways that I was taught tolerance by my parents, and I have repeated with my children:

- To be observant of my own attitudes and by demonstrating respect for others. By thinking about the behaviour, I want to see in my children and modelling those behaviours.
- By remembering that children are always listening, and they are 'sponges', they will imitate what they see and hear.

Of Lessons Learnt and Lessons Taught

- Always answer any questions they have honestly and respectfully. They will notice differences in people, and it is ok to discuss these if done in a respectful way.
- They will become exposed to unfair stereotyping at school and in the media. Always discuss these with your children, in an honest and respectful way.
- Help your child to feel good about themselves, to feel accepted, respected and valued.
- Teach them that having tolerance of others' values and beliefs does not mean the same as tolerating unacceptable behaviours.

Seasons of My Life

Care

'One person caring about another represents life's greatest value.'
- Jim Rohn

'Too often we underestimate the power of a touch, a smile, a kind word, a listening ear, an honest ear or the smallest act of caring, all of which have the potential to turn a life around.'
- Leo Buscaglia

Care of yourself and care for others can change not only yourself but those around you. To care for others, you must first care for yourself both physically and psychologically.

How to guide your child to be a caring individual:

- Believe that your child is capable of being kind and caring. If you start to believe and say they are up to 'no good' then they will soon be 'up to no good.'
- Always be a positive role model to your child.
- Practice caring in play activities with your child: in role-model scenarios, make them fun, interactive and relatable for your child.
- Be respectful of your child and their feelings.
- Let them know that how they treat others really does matter.
- Applaud and acknowledge them when they demonstrate a caring behaviour.

How have I shown and taught this to my children, by example. They have seen me strive to be caring, kind and respectful. To look after

Of Lessons Learnt and Lessons Taught

myself. To tend to them, care for them, be respectful of them. To reach out and care for family, friends and strangers. To 'be there for someone.'

Seasons of My Life

Kindness

*'A kind gesture can reach a wound
that only compassion can heal'
- Steve Maraboli*

*'No act of kindness, no matter how small, is ever wasted'
- Aesop*

Teaching and learning kindness is about showing it, and being a positive role model, whether it be through empathy, acceptance, kind gestures, or thoughtfulness.

Kindness can be a chain reaction; someone has done something kind to you and all you want to do is 'pay it forward.'

Being kind is also about love, about being selfless, caring, empathic and compassionate. Sharing love with others through kind acts such as a smile, a nice word, an unexpected deed or a planned surprise.

We all make mistakes; we are, after all, human. However, we can be kind in response to ourselves and others when those mistakes are made.

Teaching Kindness to Children:

- Be an example for your child. If you live by example, your child will follow. Remember they look up to you for guidance and mimic until they understand.
- Encourage and instil good habits such as good manners, showing gratitude, compassion or doing random acts of kindness.
- Teach them about sharing and caring.

- Discuss with them about how they feel when they have been kind to others. Focus on the positive, how good and fulfilled it made them feel.

Examples could include:

- Opening a door for someone else.
- Checking in on a neighbour's well-being. Offering to do their lawns, clean the car, and fetch their groceries when they are unable to.
- Cooking a meal for someone in need.
- Sharing what you have with others.
- Donating to charity or helping to raise money for worthwhile causes.

Purpose

'The purpose of life is to live it, to taste experience to the utmost, to reach out eagerly and without fear for newer and richer experience.'
- Eleanor Roosevelt

'You were put on this earth to achieve your greatest self, to live out your purpose and to do it courageously.'
- Jim Rohn

We should all have purpose in our lives.

Purpose means many things to many people. For me, it encompasses having goals and working towards achieving them both in personal life and professional life.

It starts when your children reach the age of wanting to do things. Things as simple as painting or drawing, reading a book, buying something they want for themselves, doing well in sport or school. I have always encouraged my children to work towards their goals but not to rush as the reward of feeling pride and developing self-worth loses its importance.

At school and in every endeavour in life I have also always encouraged them to: "Do your best, be your best," so that at the end of the day they felt they had given their project as much as they were able. That I was proud of them for having a go.

Teach by example, by living your own life with intention, by setting goals that interest you, keep you motivated and are achievable and relevant.

Of Lessons Learnt and Lessons Taught

Teach them to find purpose in their own world. As a young child this would be their home and their family then extending to their larger environment and the world around them as they grow. Teach them that just because they may initially fail or make mistakes to look on it as a learning experience. To not give up, to keep trying and then make a big deal of it when they succeed.

Some examples:

- Work on a simple family tree and who each person was, what they did and why they are important.
- Hire them for simple jobs around the house. Do a chore list with rewards for job completed. This could be monetary, a special outing or a treat.
- With an older child or teenager create a mind map with them around who they are, what they want to do, what they want to be, what they care about, how they want the world to be.
- Show interest in their goals, their ambitions and always positively encourage them.

Self-Reliance

'Long-term we must begin to build our internal strengths. It isn't just skills like computer technology. It's the old-fashioned basics of self-reliance, self-motivation, self-reinforcement, self-discipline, self-command.'
- Steven Pressfield

'When we protect our children from every source of possible danger, we also prevent them from having the kinds of experiences that develop their sense of self-reliance, their ability to assess and mitigate risk and their sense of accomplishment.'
- Gever Tulley

Self-reliance for me is the ability to do things and make decisions by yourself, without fear, with strength, a willingness to take a risk, and a belief in your own abilities.

It starts with teaching your children simple things at an age when they can achieve this.

As a toddler:

- Brushing their own teeth.
- Feeding themselves using utensils.
- Learning to dress themselves.
- Washing their own hands.
- Some independent play in short increments.

As parents we want to jump in and do everything for them, it is truly beneficial to hold back and take the extra time to allow your child to master self-reliance. Be sure to praise their efforts and

Of Lessons Learnt and Lessons Taught

balance helping them when needed with encouraging them to do it on their own.

As your child gets older and they are dealing with more complex life skills, continue to encourage, support, praise and work towards their goals, only stepping in when asked and encourage them not to be afraid of asking for help.

A great example of self-reliance and purpose for me now is writing this first book.

Having never written a book before I needed help with Structure, relevant content, and all things publishing.

I did at first feel scared and doubtful; however, because I have a firm belief in myself and my abilities, I soon put this to one side and said, "Go for it, you have got this."

Seasons of My Life

Change

'Dreams are the seeds of change. Nothing ever grows without a seed, and nothing ever changes without a dream.'
- Debby Boon

'Incredible change happens in your life when you decide to take control of what you have power over instead of craving control over what you don't.'
- Steve Maraboli

We all go through various changes in life from total dependence on our parents, to learning how to do simple things for ourselves, to education, relationships, independence, raising families of our own, loss, grief, moving house and the list goes on.

My family and I have gone through many of these things.

When young, children can be quite upset and confused by change, so it is important to take the time to listen to them, show compassion and guide them to a better understanding, particularly with the changes that occur around loss and grief.

Change can also be good; we have all heard and probably used the phrase, 'Change is good for the soul.' What the heck does this mean I can hear!

For me, it means:

- Change can help us to grow emotionally, mentally and spiritually.
- It keeps us fresh and open to new ventures and possibilities.

Of Lessons Learnt and Lessons Taught

- Being able to see something from a different perspective so that you can see the world around you in a new and refreshing way.
- It can help you reach your goals.
- It can open your mind to a new way of thinking.
- It can make life more interesting.
- It helps you to understand more fully what truly makes you happy.
- It helps you learn how to prepare and manage all situations you will encounter in your life.

When teaching your child about change:

- Talk with them about the change and involve them in any decision making.
- If able, give them time to prepare.
- Listen to and acknowledge their fears.
- Help them with ways of expressing their feelings around change, do a drawing, write it down, keep a journal.
- Teach by example, show how you handle change in positive ways.
- Keep up the communication with them throughout the process.
- Teach them that change can also be good.

Afterword

As I sit here writing the last few words of my story, I look up at a cross stitch done many years ago by my mother. It sits on the wall just inside our front door and holds an ancient Celtic verse by an unknown author. These words have always resonated with me.

It is a traditional way of wishing someone good luck and fortune on their journey through life.

> *'May the Road rise up to meet you.*
> *May the wind be always at your back.*
> *May the sun shine warm upon your face,*
> *the rains fall soft upon your fields,*
> *and until we meet again,*
> *May God hold you in the palm of His hand.'*

This has led me to ponder on what final message I would leave for my family, future generations and all who may read this book:

Seasons of My Life

*May your journey be long,
And your foot fall softly upon your own path.
May you walk each day with strength of purpose,
And meet each challenge with knowledge and a will to embrace it.
May you be true to yourself,
May you build your 'village' and embrace your life,
And most of all,
May your journey forward be filled with hope and joy in your heart.
- Anne James*

Acknowledgements

There are people and organisations that I would like to acknowledge; during my journey so far, each of them has played a significant part in supporting me and my family.

Firstly, to my 'village,' having supportive extended family and close friends has been so important. You have all cared, shown compassion and love, and have always been there to listen.

The doctors, nurses and staff, Royal Hobart Hospital ICU, for their wonderful, dedicated care of Dad during his time there, and their compassionate support of my family.

To RSL Tasmania, your care, compassion and respect for my dad on his passing, for the beautiful 'Poppy Service' that you organised, and for your care and support for my mum, both during Dad's illness and in the aftermath of his passing, was so appreciated.

Seasons of My Life

Bears of Hope (http:/www.bearsofhope.org.au) in support of Lockie, his partner and extended family. Such a dedicated and compassionate group who gave freely of their support in the aftermath of Hunter's passing.

And finally, to my wonderful Rheumatologist, so professional, knowledgeable, experienced, open, honest, caring and supportive. I could not have managed this particular challenge in my life without you.

About the Author

Anne James was born in Hobart, Tasmania. Her early childhood was one of a nomadic life as her family travelled from state to state and one time overseas following her father who was in the Armed services.

Change and adapting to new schools, and making friends came easily to Anne thanks to her parents who were progressive for their generation, and very caring and inclusive.

Anne enjoyed her education and was a bit of an academic. She continues to love reading, music, and exercising her brain.

Anne's chosen profession was that of a nurse and she worked across a number of disciplines, settling finally in general practice as a chronic disease nurse and patient educator, taking a special interest in respiratory disease, where she taught and helped her patients with their daily management. She was invited at one

Seasons of My Life

time to be a guest speaker by the Lung Foundation of Australia to present a COPD training session for nurses.

Anne has a strong love of family and is caring and nurturing. She loves nature and animals of all kinds, having a number of cats, dogs and even a budgerigar or two over the years. These days her 'pets' are the wildlife around her.

She spends her days now gardening, cooking, doing craft work and enjoying time with her family. Her belief in a strong, caring environment in which to bring up children and nurture their core values is what eventually led her to the writing of this book.

Anne James is the author of 'Seasons of My Life.' With over forty years of experience as a Registered Nurse, working across various disciplines, she ultimately moved to General Practice nursing. She pioneered and oversaw nurse-led clinics focused on managing chronic health conditions within this practice. Anne's personalised one-on-one sessions with clients were designed to address their concerns and effectively empower them to manage their chronic health conditions.

She diligently upskilled her professional development by attending courses and seminars on Asthma, COPD (Chronic Obstructive Pulmonary Disease), Diabetes, Heart Disease management and Arthritis. Anne's expertise has been recognised, and she had the privilege to present at a Lung Foundation training day for nurses, specifically focusing on COPD management.

Her unwavering passion lies in helping individuals comprehend the impact of a chronic health diagnosis on their lives, guiding them to overcome obstacles and achieve realistic, tangible goals. Nowadays, Anne aspires to empower individuals with the knowledge and tools to embrace a 'Live Well' mindset while living with their chronic health conditions.

Chronic Health Conditions – Healthy Mindset
- Knowledge is Power
- Unlocking Support Networks
- How to Reframe Your Diagnosis

Rewrite Your Health Story
- Discover Your Motivations
- Finding clarity and new progress
- Adapt & Conquer

Become a Wellness Warrior
- Shatter Limitations
- You First! Unleash Your Creativity
- Innovate as You Go…

0436 007 765   ajames60@gmail.com   www.annejamesauthor.com

Notes

www.ingramcontent.com/pod-product-compliance
Lightning Source LLC
Chambersburg PA
CBHW030300100526
44590CB00012B/463